SPIRITUAL EYES

To All Who Desire
To Gain Spiritual Sight

SPIRITUAL EYES

YANG HOON HAN

Translated by
SUNG KYUNG CHUNG

YUHA PUBLISHING COMPANY

SPIRITUAL EYES

Copyright © 2020 by Yang-Hoon Han

Published in 2020 by Yuha Publishing Company, Seoul.
Registration: 2014.04.24 387-3190000251002000000035
First edition: November 2020
ISBN: 979-11-85927-37-4

All rights reserved.
No part of this publication may be reproduced, scanned, or distributed
in any printed or electronic form without permission except for
brief quotations in printed reviews, without the prior permission of the publisher.

Cover and interior design by Da Min Chung
Printed in Korea

This book is dedicated to
those whose spiritual eyes are opened, and to those
all wish to open their spiritual eyes.

PREFACE
Korean Edition

I have realized something over the past eight years in my spiritual ministry. That is, there are many around us who want to know God deeply, engaged in spiritual warfare with Satan, and interested in healing ministry. As a minister, I had a great reward in meeting and fellowshipping with them as well as solving spiritual problems together.

First of all, I thank the Lord for helping to run so far without being aware or fearful of my surroundings in a spiritually barren environment.

Last year, I had busy days in ministry, but I was able to publish three books: they are *Heal my Lambs, Jesus Christ and His Ministry,* and *Biblical Spirituality.* This year, besides issuing the second revised edition of *Heal my Lambs,* I am releasing my fourth book, *Spiritual Eyes,* an autobiographical one. I came to publish this book to share my spiritual journey since many people were always curious about how I opened my spiritual eyes.

I expect this book to contribute big or little to readers who desire spiritual gifts and who want to serve as faithful workers of the

PREFACE

Lord. I show my appreciation to secretary So-Jin Lee for helping me with this book.

Yang-Hoon Han

May 7, 2012
Cheongnyong, Seoul, South Korea

PREFACE
English Edition

I am very pleased that my fourth book, *Spiritual Eyes,* has been translated into English and passed on to English-speaking readers. This book was released to the world eight years ago, and I believe this book has been of little help to those who yearn for spiritual things. I experienced the spiritual world in 2004, 16 years ago from now, and after receiving the gifts from God, I have devoted myself to spiritual ministry until today.

In the meantime, I have been far from the world but stepped deeper into God, the kingdom of God, and the spiritual world. I am deeply grateful to God for allowing joyful and meaningful days in the midst of numerous ministries.

It has always been my wish to see more spiritual people appear in these last days. And I believe this book will play a big part in making my wish come true.

In particular, I would like to thank Sung-Kyung Chung, who was willing to translate this book, and Da-Min Chung, who was in charge of editing and designing this book, following the last book *Biblical Spirituality.* Also, I would like to show my appreciation to

PREFACE

president Dong-In Lee of Ins P&B for his hard work in printing and producing 27 books over the past ten years.

Yang-Hoon Han

November 1, 2020
Banghwa, Seoul, South Korea

CONTENTS

• PREFACE vii

PART I – IN A SPIRITUAL ENVIRONMENT

CHAPTER 1	Born into the World 3
CHAPTER 2	My Father and Sister Fall Sick 7
CHAPTER 3	Devote to Religious Life 11
CHAPTER 4	Accommodate Patients 17
CHAPTER 5	In a Spiritual Whirlwind 19
CHAPTER 6	My Father Plants a Church 27
CHAPTER 7	Prepare to Become a Minister 29

PART II – GET TO KNOW THE SPIRITUAL WORLD

CHAPTER 8	Into the Grace of God 43
CHAPTER 9	Cry Out for Repentance and Holiness 51
CHAPTER 10	Encounter Evil Spirits 55
CHAPTER 11	Start a Pastoral Ministry 59
CHAPTER 12	Work at the Prayer House 69
CHAPTER 13	Spiritual Transition 75

PART III – ENTER INTO THE SPIRITUAL WORLD

CHAPTER 14	Spiritual Pilgrimage 87

CONTENTS

CHAPTER 15	Open Spiritual Eyes	97
CHAPTER 16	Spiritual Heritage	115
CHAPTER 17	Start a Healing Ministry	121
CHAPTER 18	Establish Siloam Mission	135
CHAPTER 19	Parting and Separation	137

PART IV – ADD DEPTH TO SPIRITUALITY

CHAPTER 20	Spiritual Exploration	147
CHAPTER 21	Spirituality and Spiritual Gifts	159
CHAPTER 22	Go Through Repentance Again	165

PART V – EXPANSION OF MINISTRY

CHAPTER 23	Begin to Explore Spiritual Sites	189
CHAPTER 24	Start a Live Bible Study	193
CHAPTER 25	Develop Various Spiritual Diagnostic Tools	197
CHAPTER 26	Fellowship with Spiritual People	201
CHAPTER 27	Begin to Write Books	203
CHAPTER 28	Establish the Siloam House	207

PART I

IN A SPIRITUAL ENVIRONMENT

CHAPTER 1

BORN INTO THE WORLD

Born in a Mud Hut

The Korean War left many scars on every family living in the Republic of Korea, and our family was no exception. My parents lived in Cheongdan, Gyeonggi-do, which is located just south of the 38th parallel that divided the South and the North before the war broke out. My parents had no connection with the area; they originally lived in Yeonbaek, near Haeju, North Korea. However, to escape from the North Korean regime's rule, they descended to the south and temporarily stayed at Cheongdan.

As North Korea invaded South Korea, my mother continued to stay in Cheongdan while my father was arrested by the North Korean soldier and was saved from the brink of death; he fled to Busan via Seoul and stayed there for two years. Having found some stability, he tried to find my mother, but the two were unable to reunite because the Cheongdan region was in the hands of North Korea. My father worked in Busan and Incheon to make money and later moved to Yongmi Island, near the 38th parallel on the west coast, which South Korea occupied, the closest area to North

Korea, to take my mother.

One day before the beginning of the spring of 1952, when South and North Korea reached an intense standoff, my father succeeded in bringing my mother to Yongmi Island by sending an acquaintance. The physical distance between the two was more than 100 kilometers. Finally, they could have a dramatic reunion after living far apart for two years. My father's incident of taking my mother out of the enemies' land was many friends' envy, for few of those who left their wives in the North reunited with their wives. My brother was three years old at the time, and I was in my mother's womb.

Months later, as North Korea took Yongmi Island, my family sneaked down into South Korea in the middle of the night on a boat. Most people who came down in this way have arrived at Incheon Harbor, yet my family arrived in Oepo-ri, Naega-myeon, Ganghwa-gun, Incheon. As a result, I was conceived in Yongmi Island, where my parents had no connection and were born in a strange place that had nothing to do with my family.

My father had settled near a Gochon reservoir beyond a hilltop. He made a hut on the empty ground before the reservoir was formed. With the locals' help, we were able to get the precious wood and other materials needed to build a house. My mother delivered me on the straw, and I was born the second son of my family. In early March, when there was still a cold wind, I was born in a strange land during the Korean War, which my mother always felt sorry for me.

Move out from Grand Parents' House

My family, who spent a year there, moved to Sangam-dong, Seoul, where my uncle lived, and my aunt also lived nearby. My maternal grandfather lived near the coastal region called Yeonan, but my uncle studied in Seoul and owned some land there. Although my mother's main family is from the Yeonan area, and she was born and raised there, emotionally, she was almost Seoulite, and all her relatives were a native of Seoul.

My family naturally lived at my mother's uncle's house, but we had to leave the house after several months because of me. I cried a lot while living there. My mother, who was in her early twenties at the time, carried me on her back and slept since the little child cried day and night unceasingly. After all, my mother's aunt suggested moving to another place, unable to endure the noise.

When I think about it now, I might have cried a lot as a baby because I was conceived and born in wartime. My mother and I must have been very anxious by the shouting of soldiers, gunshots, and the sound of cannon. Unfortunately, I was brought up in the midst of fighting from a fetus.

When I diagnosed myself spiritually, there were many spirits of depression. My mother was very lonely when she conceived me, away from her husband for two years, and grieved because she did not know whether the husband was dead or alive. My mother's emotions and state of mind at the time had a significant impact on me. I must have cried all the time, being depressed and oversensitive at small things.

Another reason may be because my maternal family's spiritual environment was not particularly good. My grandfather's younger brother died of illness before our family moved out, and his son, my mother's cousin, also died of an explosion accident. Later I realized that the house had many evil spirits, such as the spirit of murder and the spirit of despair.

Another heartbreaking story is that one of my uncles, who was in an important office at the transportation department, died of illness at the age of forty. He was fond of me and paid for my tuition. Many relatives died in vain at such a young age. My maternal family was well-off and wealthy, yet they had many issues to resolve spiritually.

Set Permanent Address and Register my Birth

My family left my mother's uncle's house and moved into my mother's aunt's house nearby. However, the spiritual environment was not very good, either. My family ended up leaving the house within a few months. Just as Abraham left his people and his father's household, we had to leave and had nowhere to settle.

We moved to Daehyeon-dong, Seoul, where many of my father's friends were, and he built a small house there. My parents set my permanent address here and registered my birth that they had postponed. I finally became a citizen of the Republic of Korea.

I went to Shinhyeon Church in Daehyeon-dong when I was three or four years old, and my brother entered a nearby elementary school. We often went to nearby Ewha Woman's University to play. Later, my father moved to Sinseol-dong to work, and we went to Changsin Church and again moved to Dapsimni soon after.

The reason we had to move was again because of me. I often fought with a house owner's son, who was of the same age, and I was always a winner. Then the adults got on bad terms, and eventually, my father decided to move out. The neighborhood where we moved had many lovely homes for the working class. It was the first time we owned a new house in Seoul, and I entered elementary school.

CHAPTER 2

MY FATHER AND SISTER FALL SICK

After moving to Dapsimni, my father had many different jobs to support the family. He suffered from neuralgia, and his lungs got bad even before he turned forty. I was anxious and depressed to see him suffer from illness at an early age. To complete my misfortune, my younger sister, who was four years old, caught diphtheria, a disease legally designated as an epidemic. We were on alert, and she was admitted to a pediatric ward in Seoul, but her condition worsened, and some children hospitalized with the same disease died. We could not help but fear the worst situation.

My sister's medical attendants told my father in passing that he could import a cure directly from the United States if we can afford it. We sold our house in a hurry and set aside the cost of her treatment, and we were able to save her life. What good medicine could there have been in Korea in the late 1950s, not long after the war? Had it not been for the love of my father, raising money by selling the house to save his daughter, my sister probably would not have recovered from the illness.

At that time, we suffered from the sickness of my father and sister and the financial difficulties. One time, my father spent a lot of money digging a well in the yard, but he lost money because there was no water. Besides that, we suffered from many financial difficulties due to big and small problems. I always questioned why my family, the children of God, had to go through such hardships. It was not until my spiritual eyes are opened that I could answer my question.

I made a visit to the house with my disciples for the first time in fifty years after my spiritual eyes are opened to examine the house spiritually. Although many years had passed, the house remained the same. I was astonished to see a shrine to the village deity right next to my house, and I was again amazed at the size of evil spirits; they were stretching out from the shrine and affecting my house. My family and other people who have lived in this house must not have lived an easy life.

According to the book, *Exorcism and Shamanism of Korea* written by Rusi Hwang, the shrine next to my house was one of Seoul's top three shrines. Imagine how powerful the evil spirits would have been!

I lived in the area for eight years. Every year the villagers collected money and performed an exorcism at the shrine. Fortunately, my family went to church, so we did not participate in the ritual and did not eat the ritual food. Besides my family, only a few families in the town were not involved in the shaman ritual.

My father believed there would be nothing to fear for we are in Christ, but since we lived so close to the shrine, we were severely attacked by evil forces. I often played on the spot, knowing nothing. Even when the door was closed, my friends and I somehow managed to get into the shrine and played; the mere thought of it, I get goosebumps. Having played in such a place with so many dark spirits, I had no choice but to be attacked frequently.

CHAPTER 3

DEVOTE TO RELIGIOUS LIFE

When I was in elementary school, I attended Dapsimni Methodist Church. My father was baptized in the Methodist Church when he was young. We chose the church because it was the closest one, about a hundred meters away. As the Dapsimni Church gradually revived, we built a new church building in the upper part of our neighborhood.

Although I attended a Sunday school, I was not very religious. A Seventh-day Adventist Church in our neighborhood distributed candies and snacks to children, and I also went there several times to get sweets.

One of my friends picked me up every Sunday when I was in fourth grade. He was the son of elder Park, who lived only 50 meters away. He and I went to the same school, and we were in the same grade. He was good at studying, and he also won first prize at Sunday school. He later graduated from Seoul National University, one of the best universities in Korea, and worked at a broadcasting station. He became a celebrity by writing lyrics for a Dokdo song, which is a small island in the East Sea of Korea.

At that time, Christianity was on its rise, and many churches were built, and the number of saints increased. But Korea still had few homes that did not hold ancestral rites under the influence of Confucianism. South Korea used to keep track of students' religious status at school. Assuming that there were about 80 to 90 students in a class, on average, 30 to 40 students were Buddhists, while Christians were only five. Although Christianity was growing, it was quite awkward for students to raise their hands and say that they are Christians.

Attend Another Church

My family was attending Dapsimni methodist church, which built a new building in the upper neighborhood, and the presbyterian church moved into the previous building. My older brother told me that many people follow the young and competent evangelist of the presbyterian church.

For some reason or another, my father attended the presbyterian church; he served as a deacon. He was passionate enough to take the lead when something difficult happened in the church. Most of the saints were either students or young people, so our house was almost always packed with guests. The evangelist in charge of the church took lodging at our home for months, and my mother did her best to serve him. He later became a general assembly president of the Jesus Korea Holiness Church.

As the church went through some affairs, many saints came out of the church and established the Damsimni holiness church with the evangelist. I happened to experience methodist, presbyterian, and holiness church in the short term. Although I graduated from a Presbyterian seminary, I reject denominationalism. I do believe that the church should be one. The reason why I had an interest and had cooperated with the ecumenical movement may be due to my spiritual background as a child.

Feel Special

By the time I was in middle school, my family served God very fervently and was loyal to the church. The early and mid-1960s was a period when the fire of revival was raging in Korean churches. God also gave a zeal of faith in the heart of my family. My brother, as well as my parents, almost lived in the church; although we were not a minister, we had a heart of minister; we loved the church.

By the time I entered middle school, I often felt special before God and wanted to live differently from others. I not only went to church every week but also tried to live godly in my daily life.

At that time, doggy dance and other dances were popular among teenagers. My neighborhood friends smoked, drank, and danced a lot. I thought my friends were immature, so I never danced and played with them. I did not drink, smoke, or read comic books either. Also, except for going to the movies as a group at school, I went to see a movie with my friends only a few times. I restrained myself from playing baseball, soccer, and table tennis which were my favorite activities. One may think my temperance is too much and may even ask if it is necessary. Yet, I felt that all of this was somehow secular, and I could not behave like my friends. Therefore, I tried to abstain from worldly pleasures and lived in the church on Sunday, which I enjoyed the most.

My parents never told me to study hard throughout my secondary school years. Instead, my mother told me to turn off the light and go to bad if I stayed up late into the night studying. Every time, my parents instructed me to attend church and live according to God's word faithfully. I have no idea why my parents raised and taught me in this way, but in consequence, I became a pastor, and all five of my brothers and sisters studied theology, and most of them serve God as a pastor now.

My Father Devotes Himself to Prayer

Throughout my teenage years, my father ran a rice business near Sindap Station, Dapsimni. It was a relatively large store with a combination of wholesale and retail. At the same time, he was a faithful deacon in the church. From day one, he left the store to my older brother, often emptied the shop, and went to the mountain to pray. As a businessman, it was not an easy thing to do. I was too young to understand why my father often went to the mountain to pray.

My father first went to a church in his hometown when he was seven years old. He said that he was the first person in the region to attend the church. As young, he did not drink and smoke. He was faithful to his family and committed to church life; he was different from the average adult.

One time, a shocking incident occurred; my father attempted to kill himself. He often went to Samgak Mountain, a famous place for spiritual energy, and he held onto a tree on a high rock while praying. In the 1960s, it was fashionable to hold a pine tree and pray among Korean believers. People thought that only then could they receive great power. Revivalist also stressed that the saints should pray hard enough to pull out a pine tree.

My father was no exception. He prayed that he would let go of his hands, holding the tree if God does not grant his wishes. However, God did not respond to my father's threatening words, and he indeed let go of his hands. My father, of course, fell under the rock and lost his consciousness. Passing hikers found him and transferred him to the Dongbu Municipal Hospital. The hospital determined that my father had died already, so they placed him in a morgue without any treatment. Surprisingly, he came to consciousness himself and returned home in three days. My father testified that he died and came back to life again.

I saw my mother washing a bloodstained suit in the yard when I came back from school. She gave me a brief explanation of what had happened because I was panicking. When I entered the room, I saw his back head broken, and there was dirt everywhere. Although he was injured, my father never went to the hospital since he came back; he only applied Mercurochrome.

Many years after, this episode of my father became known to many Christians in South Korea. It was my father who was the main character of the story, "There was a man who fell from a tree and died while praying in Samgak Mountain, but came back to life in three days."

Although he went through a tough time, my father continued to pray on the mountain. He fasted often and prayed alone in the cold in the middle of winter. During winter, the temperature usually dropped below minus 20 degrees celsius. It is common sense that mountains are colder than cities. Imagine how cold it must have been! There was no shelter in the mountain at that time. My father washed his clothes and bathed while the sun was out. At all events, he received great power and came down from the mountain.

My father closed the rice shop, sold his house, moved to Sanggye-dong, and moved again to Pyeongchang-dong. This house belonged to Samgak Mountain Church. I guess he had decided to work at the Samgak Mountain Church while praying at Samgak Mountain. Just a year after my father devoted himself to prayer, he began to be recognized as a man of God among people around.

CHAPTER 4

ACCOMMODATE PATIENTS

My father loved to pray for the sick, and it worked. One day I came back from school, and a middle-aged woman was sitting in my room. I heard that the lady was demon-possessed. She talked incoherently and made unusual body movements. Sometimes she gathered her hands, raised her index finger to form a pointed figure, and then circled around the room in every nook and cranny. This woman came to our house to receive healing. After a week, she was cured and went home. Shortly afterward, we could hear good news about her. The lady was given the ability to cast out demons after being freed from the evil spirits, so she started her own healing ministry.

Once, a handsome young man stayed with our family. My father prayed for his mental illness for a long period of time. I spent months sharing my room with this young man, but he was not fully recovered as far as I remember.

My father often told us the fruits of his healing ministry. When he prayed for cancer patients or diabetic patients, they often received complete healing. I still remember him more as a rice seller than as a healing minister. However, at that time, the life of my father was transitioning from a trader to a healing minister. Those who had been healed took my father to town and bought him suits or shoes as gifts. Many saints who were cured or heard about our family helped us financially in times of economic hardship.

CHAPTER 5

IN A SPIRITUAL WHIRLWIND

A Poisonous Snake Bites

About six months after my father became a healing minister, I was in my third year of middle school. One afternoon in October, I went up the mountain in the back of the village to pick some Chinese pepper with my younger sister because it added a nice flavor to chueotang, a loach in hot bean paste soup; it also went well with soybean paste. Previously, I lived only in a residential area in Seoul, so it was the first time going up to the mountain. We could easily pick up a Chinese pepper by merely climbing the hill for a few minutes. I found it in the valley, so we went into the bush, but all of a sudden, I felt pain on top of my left foot. Since we were in the bush, I thought I was stuck in the thorns, but the pain grew stronger as time went by.

I quickly came out of the bush and took off my socks. There were two holes in my foot. The moment I saw blood and yellow pus, I knew I was bitten by a poisonous snake. I was told to tie the top of the wound with a cord when bitten by a venomous snake, but I could not find a suitable one around me, so I jumped home in a whirl without tying my legs. As soon as I got back, I bound my left ankle tight with a strap.

Within a few minutes, however, my left foot swelled, and my mind faded. I laid on the floor, struggling with pain all over my body. My older brother saw me and ran to the local pharmacy, and my mother was so surprised that she kept praying next to me. After an hour, my brother came back with empty-hands crying. When he went to the pharmacy, the pharmacist said he had no antidote. So he ran to a nearby hospital, but doctors also said they could not treat patients like me. My brother cried hard because he thought I was going to die, and I faced a fearful situation that was so ridiculous.

My brother called father immediately because he was leading a meeting in a church in Sangye-dong. My brother told him that I was on the verge of death, but he replied, "I will return home after the meeting because if he is destined to die, there is nothing I can do for him even if I go home now." I was dumbfounded at his answer, and the anxiety was at its height. For me, it was hard to understand my father's behavior. Since he had a great healing gift, I expected him to come and heal me as soon as possible. But eventually, my father came home the next day.

I suffered unbearable pain that evening. My mother informed the church that a poisonous snake had bitten me. Just then, there was a meeting going on, and about 500 saints prayed for me. I could hear the sound of their prayer lying at home. The saints' prayers helped me in my anxiety, and their prayers were like a doctor and medicine to me.

That night is remembered as the most painful night of my life. I was sick all over, so I could not lie still for even ten seconds. I was groaning in pain all night; I stayed up without taking any painkillers, nutritional supplements, or an antibiotic. No one took the poison out of my foot or treated me.

When people heard that I was dying, they came to my house and said many things. Some said, "A person who was bitten by a snake on the same spot died last year," and others said, "He can live if he survives tonight." Only a year ago, my father fell on a rock and nearly died, and now I was in danger of my life. Mountain Samgak has become a place of great hardship for our family.

I made up my mind to survive, no matter what. Then I prayed to the Lord: "Lord, save me, and I will work for your kingdom." It was a moment of a fifteen-year-old boy dedicating the rest of his life for the kingdom of God. If I make a promise that I would work for God, I thought he might preserve my life. Until then, I just wanted to become famous like everyone else. But I set a clear goal that night: "Let's survive and serve God!"

The night, which seemed never to end passed, and it became morning. Watching the sunrise gave me strength. I remembered the word that I would live if I survive the night. It gave me great hope at the moment. I do not know the exact time, but my father came home. If I had died last night, he would have had my funeral, but by the grace of God, I was alive.

My father brought an adult who can do acupuncture from the neighborhood. He pricked my left foot hundreds of times with a needle and drew blood. Then as a folk remedy, he applied bean leaf on the spot. My parents did not take me to the hospital; instead, I was treated at home for many days. I had a forthcoming high school entrance exam, but I could not go to school for two weeks.

Give up on Planting Church

I failed to enter the high school that I aimed for, so I took another year. I studied in the library, but most of the time, I usually studied at home. But my heart burned day by day with a passion for the Lord rather than studying for the exam. The thought lingered in my head that I was alive because I swore to God that I would be a servant of the Lord.

There are a few other surrounding elements that aroused my desire for the Lord. Since our house was located at the foot of the mountain in Pyeongchang-dong, where many people came around to pray on the mountain, the sound of people praying resounded all over the neighborhood. When I went out at night, I could often see people holding onto trees near my house and praying eagerly in tongues all night. In addition, those who visited my house to associate with my father were very enthusiastic people. They were experts in the Bible or had many spiritual gifts, and among them, many fasted for 40 days. My father also became more deeply entrenched in the Lord as he had fellowship with great men and women of God. Naturally, his spiritual ability grew stronger, and had more insight into the word of God.

Our family was economically difficult, but spiritually we grew up considerably and got closer to the Lord. Since our church often invited famous speakers to hold revival meetings, we often heard many great sermons of famous evangelists. As a result, every time I attended a revival meeting, my desire to serve God grew.

Since I had promised to God to become his servant and had enough passion in my heart, I read the Bible diligently and prayed hard. I especially enjoyed talking to spiritual people about the spiritual world or spirituality. Most of those who attended our church at that time and had fellowship with our family have become great pastors afterward.

Then one day, I met an evangelist who set fire to my heart. He said that this is the end of time saying, "There is not much time left before the Lord returns." Then he rebuked people for putting their interest in worldly things. I was impatient to hear that because there were still many people in the world who did not know God.

The Christian population in Korea was less than 10 percent of the total population at that time. I thought to myself, 'What will happen to people who had no chance to hear the gospel if the second coming of Christ is near?' I felt so sorry for those souls. I could not stand at the thought that there are too many places in Korea where there are no churches and no pastors at all. With this as a momentum, I decided to serve God in a rural area where the gospel had not been preached yet and where there is no church to attend.

I decided to go to the valley of Gangwon province to share the gospel. Inspired by my enthusiasm, one of our church's high school students joined me. My friend suggested to drop-out of school together. It was the hot summer of August, and we proceeded without delay to get ready to leave. I prepared several Bibles, numerous other books, and supplies. I made up my mind to leave no matter what people say.

My parents and older brother tried to stop me, they asked, "Where are you going? What can you do?" But I was firm in my determination. On the day I decided to leave with my friend, my twenty-year-old brother grabbed me by the collar and hit me. I told him not to hinder me from leaving home for the Lord.

My father reluctantly made the last proposal to meet the head of the Samgak First Prayer Mountain before I take off. He persuaded, "If the head agrees with you, I will also allow you to leave and even support you financially." I accepted his suggestion because I respected him. The head acknowledged my passion but said I am way too young. He convinced me that he would help if I go on a mission after graduating from the seminary. I had a tough time accepting his opinion because it will take at least seven more years, and then I had to join the military as every other Korean man, which will take another two to three years. It was disappointing that I had to wait another decade to get to the missionary work. My heart was in a hurry thinking, 'What if the Lord comes to judge before that time?' But I was persuaded by the word of the head whom I respected, and eventually returned home and unpacked my luggage.

Experience Conversion

I was baptized at seventeen, according to church law. In those days, before churches gave baptism, they asked questions in-depth, but the pastors did not ask me anything when they baptized me. Since my religious fervor was famous within the church, they probably have thought that there is no need for questions. My enthusiasm grew unabated over time. I was young, but I searched for the things that I could serve in the church and did my best in everything. Even though some older brothers in the church made a fool of me, my heart burned with love for the Lord.

One day at the church gathering, a guest speaker preached the passage from Isaiah, chapter 43, and verse 1: "Do not fear, for I have redeemed you; I have called you by name; you are mine!" I was greatly touched by his sermon and felt as if the word was spoken directly to me. My heart broke listening to the sermon and wept for a quite long time.

God spoke to me through Isaiah 43:1, and I was sure he called me. A few years ago, I had made a vow to become his servant, but it was my will. However, this time, it was the Lord who called me through the sermon, so it was very meaningful. I became more convinced at his calling over time. From then on, I was not owned by my parents, friends, or society. Of course, I was not my master either; I only belonged to the Lord. No one has taken charge of me since that day except the Lord. At the age of seventeen, I entirely became a man of God.

Since then, I have read and studied the word of God hard. Although the Bible commentaries were very expensive, I begged my father to buy them. When I could not understand the text, I referred to the commentary. I loved the Bible so much that I transcribed the New Testament even though I was not able to finish. I not only missed a single service and meeting but went to the revival meetings held in other churches. I was already a minister in my mind.

CHAPTER 6

MY FATHER PLANTS A CHURCH

In 1970, my father, full of grace, first established a church in Seoul. He named the church Samsung, which belonged to the Korean Presbyterian Church. A deacon who attended the same church ran a ranch and owned several houses. We purchased one of them as a church building from him, and my family moved to a small house.

My Father served the church as an evangelist while working. I heard him saying several times in his preaching that he admires Paul, who also served God's kingdom and worked as a tentmaker. Soon after, as facilities for people with disabilities were built near the church, we were compensated and moved to Seongnam. We built an 1100 square feet building on 1400 square feet of land. In 1970, it was very rare to build a church on this scale. We started building the church with the finance we had and with support from all over the place. At that time, the church was built with blocks, but the ready-made products purchased at the factory were poor in quality. So my father called an engineer to build a church with strong bricks. Sometimes I sprayed water on the blocks and carried them. I was preparing for the entrance exam, but when my father asked for help, I could not disobey him. By everyone's efforts, the church was built beautifully.

Unfortunately, there was a shaman's house right next to our church. When seen on a straight line, there was our house, someone else's house, a shaman's house, and a church building. We, sometimes, heard the beat of a drum and small gongs from the shaman's house even during the service hours. We fought a war of nerves with the shaman. When I ran into a shaman or her family on the street, I did not greet them, although we were neighbors. Later the shaman's daughter received great evil spirits and became a great shaman.

My father served the church wholeheartedly and fought a spiritual war with the shaman by praying every day. He despised people who were involved in shamanism, but since a few years ago, he started to share the gospel to shamans and fortune-tellers. I have no idea where my father got the courage to do that. When our family gathered, he shared how he evangelized and preached to them.

CHAPTER 7

PREPARE TO BECOME A MINISTER

Enter a Seminary

I graduated from high school and entered the seminary. At that time, my father was taking little time off from the ministry and had no other stable jobs. So I could not afford tuition. My family lived in Seoul most of the time, so we had no acquaintances when suddenly moved to Seongnam. We were daunted in every way than we lived in Seoul. The three years I lived there was remembered as the most challenging times of my life, both psychologically and economically.

My father strongly opposed me from entering the seminary because it was challenging to proceed to university and study at that time, but beyond that, he did not want me to become a pastor. My father wanted me to have a stable job, and live comfortably, taking care of my family. The pastor was not on the list of coveted jobs in Korean society because people thought pastors go through all sorts of hardships. Only a few people around me wanted to become a pastor. Not only my friends and acquaintances opposed me, but so did the saints when they heard the news that I was determined to become a pastor. Having set my life goal as a minister, I could not slow it down even for a moment, so I worked part-time to raise the entrance fee. I entered the seminary with difficulty without the encouragement or cooperation of my father and others.

My father did not change his mind for years. After I came back from serving in the Korean Army, I wanted to return to the seminary, but he persuaded me to give up on my study. By that time, he had a ministry in Bongcheon-dong, Seoul, but he dissuaded me from attending the seminary and kept me from involving in a ministry. However, he could not stop me because my will to live as a minister was way more firm than his opposition. This was the only time I disobeyed my father.

I lived in Seongnam and went to the seminary in Sadang-dong. It cost me a lot of time and transportation expenses than I expected. There was a bus passing near Banpo that went from Seongnam to Sadang-dong. So I often walked from Banpo to school in Sadang to save bus fare. Nevertheless, I went to school tenaciously. I had to eat breakfast before six o'clock and leave home so that I could arrive at the seminary in time for my eight o'clock class. However, on the day I had breakfast, it was difficult to arrive on time. I was often late for the first class, which was usually English or German, and was glanced at by a professor. My grades were not good because I could not do my best often feeling drained.

As I entered the seminary and suffered materially, I was greatly daunted. By the grace of God, I was called an evangelist to a church in Geoyeo-dong, and someone introduced me to a private lesson, so I could tutor a girl until I joined the army. However, it was too much to serve the church and even tutor while studying. My route was quite complicated: I went to Sadang-dong from Seongnam, where my house was located to take classes. After class, I went to Sinseol-dong, where there was a student, and came back to Seongnam in the middle of the night. On Sunday and Wednesday, I went to Geoyeo-dong, where the church was for the service. I was able to get a lot of pay because I did many things.

I received 30,000 won, about 27 dollars, a month. Comparing that the tuition for a semester was 40,000 won in the early 70s, it was quite a wage. Even though graduates of prestigious universities were anxious to have part-time jobs. It was such a great favor for me to have a private lesson as a seminary student.

I had little time to hang out with friends after school, whether church or school friends, and had no time to prepare for my classes. I got through all the hardships only with the strong desire to graduate from the seminary to become a pastor. No matter how hard it was, I never gave up on my vocation. And by God's grace, the period of material suffering ended and God provided my needs.

God always works mysteriously. While I was enduring my father's non-cooperation and material difficulties, I ran into an old neighborhood when my family lived in Pyeongchang-dong. It turned out that he was in charge of the seminary construction. He recognized me and asked my father's regards and wanted to see him. Taking this opportunity, my father got close to Pastor Hee-bo Kim, the seminary dean, and eventually worked as a staff member of our school. As a result, we moved to Seoul again, and my father continued to minister after retiring from the school. God blessed my seminary admission miraculously.

Join the Army

All Korean men are obliged to serve the country after they become adults. I joined the army at the age of 22. Looking back now, I realize that the 34 months of service as a soldier was a period of training prepared by God. I learned how to fight and win over the enemy thoroughly in the army.

Now, I am the general fighting on a spiritual battlefield. Whether it is a spiritual war or a real war, the principle and the purpose are the same: it is to protect the country and its people and you must win. If you lose a battle, you will bear irrevocable misfortune and death. Victory is the only goal of the military.

God did not just let me be at peace in the army. I originally applied to join the Air Force with a close seminary friend. However, due to a large number of applicants, I was assigned to take a test on Sunday. I, as a seminary student, could not take the exam without going to a Sunday service, so I gave up the test. On the other hand, my colleague enlisted in the Air Force and had an excellent military life.

I joined the army and received training in Nonsan. Meanwhile, I was told to write a training manual because my handwriting was pretty good. As a result, I had to miss training many times. The company commander said he would let me work here after the necessary training. I was pleased with his proposal, and many of my colleagues envied me. But when the basic military training was over, I was sent to the supplementary battalion with over a thousand people, which was very disappointing.

There, they picked me as one of three candidates who will be on the duty of assisting a high ranking officer. It was a position that everyone desired. The interviewer noted to me that I was the most influential candidate. Hearing that I expected my military life to be comfortable, but suddenly I was informed that the recruiting was canceled because somehow the predecessor was not discharged yet. I was greatly disappointed and a little upset with God.

In the end, I was assigned to a troop called Mangho, which

means a fierce tiger. The army was known for their strong discipline and high level of combat training, as they had just been out of the war in Vietnam. People felt sorry for me because I was assigned to a unit that everyone was reluctant to go to. My forlorn hope has gone away, and I was so discouraged.

As soon as I arrived at the unit, I received another two months of new training, the first of its kind at the boot camp. More than a hundred soldiers from Seoul were harshly trained. Giving up all my hope of living a comfortable military life, I wished to serve in the religious division. The unit chaplain sent me a positive signal after interviewing me, but at the end of two months of training, I had to face another ordeal. The division commander ordered all the intelligent soldiers trained this time should not be left behind in the administrative or division headquarters but should be sent to each subordinate unit to enhance the combat capability. What he said was right, but my hope went up in smoke again.

I was stationed in the battalion with 30 other colleagues. About half of the number went to the barbershop while others were waiting in front of the battalion headquarters. I was resting with remained soldiers, and some officers unexpectedly showed up and ordered to perform Taekwondo. After seeing various demonstrations, they selected four among us, including me; and informed that we are going to be sent to the artillery. It seemed like they have chosen strong soldiers with outstanding physical. We were proud of being picked by officers and assigned to the headquarter, but it did not take long to find out that it was one of the most notorious platoons.

What I learned later was that they had to supplement manpower to prepare for the upcoming divisional competition, so they selected recruits first on top of their list. Most other colleagues were assigned to other companies. I was resentful for being selected for a long time, and I blamed God a lot because my fate has changed completely in less than 30 minutes.

The highest seniority in the religious division was just about to be discharged, and he was on his way to our group to find his successor. But he was told that many of us are at the barbershop, so he had gone to the barbershop first, however, there was no seminarian there. When he came to me, I was already chosen as the artillery.

He happened to be my senior seminarian; so he asked the officer in charge of me if he can take me with him, but the officer refused the request. The officer had many other choices, but he did not change his mind. I was dumbfounded at his stubbornness. The senior met a battalion commander and a military chaplain, but all his efforts were to no avail. He told me he tried his best, but the result was not good, and he left after comforting me with few words. I had a tearful and arduous military life since then, and I could not stop thinking, 'You are so mean God!'

I cannot describe the details for security reasons, but we were trained and evaluated harshly. I had another month of hard training to death. My father, who worked at the seminary, came to see me by himself. When he saw me being trained severely, he said, "If you can't do it, say you can't do it anymore," but I decided to endure the training from start to finish. At the end of all training, several units gathered to receive training evaluations, but unfortunately, our troops came in last. It goes without saying how furious the commander of our unit was.

Without the reward of special qualification training, we returned to our camp and underwent merciless training again. The platoon commander was furious, so he pushed us further, insulting our character. Also, we barely slept at night with the aggravated backstabbing of angry commanders and senior officers. If I am correct, our troops had sound sleep only two or three days a month. I was upset with God again. The pain continued, and I fell into the bottomless pit.

Our unit was sanctioned for almost everything because of our poor performance. So it was not the atmosphere to attend church on Sunday. However, I went to church almost every Sunday despite the heavy atmosphere, including Wednesday and evening services. There was only one person in our platoon who were Christian besides me. Since I left a lot of work behind and attended church services all the time, persecution followed.

When even all units were on alert and fully armed, I still attended a Sunday daytime service. There was no one in the church except a few soldiers in the religious division, and they were all dressed in combat costumes as well. They must have thought strangely how I came to the church under these circumstances; I kept my faith risking my life and death.

One day, a high-ranking officer living outside the camp suddenly entered the unit on Sunday evening. He was angry, and he picked on me. He grabbed my cheek and dragged me around in front of several soldiers. I could not figure out why he was doing this to me.

Later, the quick-witted senior told me that he probably vented his anger on me because he was furious after fighting with his wife, who was a Christian. I cried a lot on the inside, blaming God. I do not enjoy telling negative stories although it is all in the past. However, in an unimaginably difficult atmosphere, my evening was harsher than the training during the daytime; countless nights were like hell to me. Probably other platoon members felt the same way. I wanted a smooth life in the military, but my wish did not come true.

A new platoon leader came to our unit, but he was soon reassigned as an assistant to a division commander. He visited our unit, with an intent to find a duty to serve the commander. He met the highest officer in our unit and an officer in charge because he wanted to take me. I guess I caught his eyes when I served him. He probably thought that I would assist the division commander well. A duty from the battalion headquarters came to me and said with a smile, "I think you're going to go with him today." But an hour later, I heard heartbreaking news: my leaders insisted that they would never allow me to go, so the platoon leader inevitably went back.

Since all my platoon members know this story, they always looked at me pitifully. Frankly speaking, no one would want to be in such a unit with harsh training and strict internal discipline. I have looked for a loophole many times; however, all the opportunities were wasted every once in a while.

Under the platoon leader, who refused to send me to the religious division when I was first assigned to this unit, I tasted all sorts of bitterness. Sometime after, he moved to another division within the same headquarters. One day he came to see me and said he wanted to take me with him. If he could have taken me out of my present post, why did he not send me in the first place? He did not allow me to go elsewhere because he sought his interests first, without considering my aptitude, along with the ambition of improving combat power. This time, it was again his greed to take me to his new post. I was furious, but I accepted his offer because I wanted to take a position that somehow was less painful. Unbelievably the proposal again came to naught because my current officer disapproved. Seeing every chance slip through my fingers, I cried on the inside. But God comforted me in the midst of my agony.

I was assigned to the position of calculating the distance of firing at the tactical fire direction center, which was a vital position. When several troops gathered for training, I calculated the distance precisely and got stand-down as a reward. I also won first place in the speech contest, which I was forced to participate in. I was very good at shooting, especially the night firing; I have never missed a single shot in my military career. I was also well off at double march and boxing. Most people who were hit by me bled or ran away. Those who were defeated in the boxing match called me a "gangster pastor." I was fitted well as a military person. Although I became sergeant, I kept served as a messenger of the platoon leader. I also got a lot of praise for my excellent writing in the interior class. Some seniors occasionally harassed me, but I have rarely been beaten or insulted by officers.

Many people around me jokingly recommended me to apply for the long-term service. There were many intelligent soldiers from prestigious universities in our unit, but I always stood out in many ways. I could have become a soldier if I was not called as a servant of God. Even my homeroom teacher recommended me to apply for the Military Academy when I was in high school.

As a soldier calculating the firing distance based on the map, I could not miss even a millimeter. Based on my calculation, the artillery fired guns, so if I make a mistake, it could lead to a big accident. Therefore, I learned delicacy and coolness while handling the position, and I could also learn intensity because it was a combat-resistant unit. Above all, I learned how to endure tough relationships. All of these are applicable to spiritual battles. Now that I think of it, God has equipped me with everything I need for spiritual combat during the military service.

I was in the army, but I always thought about home. I took some of my salaries off and saved six dollars for two years; I sent this money home so that my younger siblings can buy books. Our unit could take only one 25-day leave a year, but during the Christmas and New Year seasons, I was able to take two 25 days off. Everyone was jealous and said I was so lucky. After two months from my last vacation, which was New Year's Day, I was discharged. I was grateful to be able to give my parents a New Year's greeting.

Get married

When I attended middle school, I decided to become a pastor, so all my life was set for ministry. At that time, it was almost mandatory for Korean to get married culturally. I did not look for a beautiful or lovely woman in my eyes; instead, I looked for a spouse who can serve the church with me. Some of my mentors advised that my standard is improper. No matter what they said, I desired the one, who is suitable for the ministry.

Sometimes women showed interest in me, and at other times, I had eyes on them. But, when I considered each person's various aspects, I was not sure whether I can be satisfied if I choose one of them as a life partner in terms of working together for the kingdom of God. I was not very high in other standards, but I genuinely wanted to meet someone who can do the ministry together.

Without having a real date or involved in a serious relationship, I went to the army. I stood sentry almost every day, and every time I prayed for a suitable spouse. At that time, my father had retired from the seminary and was pastoring in Bongcheon-dong. I served my father's church for six months before going to another church as an educational evangelist.

There was a sister who had been in the Full Gospel Church for a long time and came to our church recently. She was passionate and volunteering; she left a good impression on my father because he valued active and zealous heart. Without asking my opinion, my father asked her to become his daughter-in-law. He probably thought that I needed a wife with an opposite personality for I was sometimes timid and passive. But she reacted passively to the proposal because I was still a student and had no ability.

We held a family meeting and agreed to some extent that it would be nice to welcome the woman as my spouse. I trusted their opinions because my parents were people who prayed a lot. It was not easy to refuse their choice because I took my parents' words as God's words.

Anyway, now the ball came over to me, and I dated her. After going on a few dates, I asked her to marry me saying, "My father likes you." In a way, it was an irresponsible and pathetic proposal. She asked me, "What about you? Do you love me?" I replied, "Although I do not know much about you, I do love you a little bit." I also told her my parents would not have made a mistake choosing his daughter-in-law. She was half-convinced, but a few weeks later, she accepted my proposal, and we got married the following year. With a stable heart, I could concentrate on my study and devote to church ministry. I was getting ready step by step to become a minister.

PART 2

GET TO KNOW THE SPIRITUAL WORLD

CHAPTER 8

INTO THE GRACE OF GOD

Receive Grace

My wife and I set up a nest in Sangdo-dong shortly after our marriage since it was close to the seminary. At that time, I was an educational evangelist at Shinsung Church in Haengdang-dong. It was a spiritual and growing church. I served the church for two years. I still remember Pastor Yong-Seo Kang's intellectual and spiritual preaching.

In the past, pastor Kang started his career at the Muhak Church in Seoul, an integrated Presbyterian church, and then pioneered the Shinsung Church. Recently, I learned that pastor Kang was the brother of pastor Doo-Sup Um's wife, a man of God I admire the most.

The knowledge I acquired in the seminary was of great help when I served the church, but through the pastors and the cultures of several churches that I served, I learned the real side of the church. I think learning theology in the church is the most basic. The theological study, far from the church, is nothing more than building castles on sand. There are two ways to get to know the church: one can be learned by staying in one church for a long time, and the other by attending several churches every two to three years. And I chose the latter.

A few months after teaching students at Shinsung Church, a prayer meeting was held every evening for 40 days. I had a lot of studies at the time, and although my home and church were far away, I went to church every day after school because of my position as an evangelist. Somehow, I did not lead the students spiritually, but they led me to a prayer meeting.

The youth leader of the church was a researcher at the Korea Advanced Institute of Science and Technology, who was a few years older than me. He had a lot of work to do and was a socially competent person, but he tried hard to pray. Among the young people, there were seminary students as well. No matter how busy I was, I could not let them get together and pray without me. Every evening we gathered together, and our prayer gradually deepened. The Holy Spirit fell on our meeting, and fervent prayer continued. It was unusual for young people to be so eager to pray.

One day when the group prayer was over, I went to the corner of the church and started to pray again passionately. While praying, I was filled by the Holy Spirit; my body suddenly became hot and strange words began to come out of my mouth. I have seen a lot of people speaking in tongues, but I have never done it. It was my first experience of speaking in tongues.

At that time, I did not consider speaking in tongues was a necessary gift. Seminaries also did not encourage it either. Some professors even taught there is no such thing as the gift of tongues anymore in this age. It was difficult for me to ignore their arguments because I respected them.

Although I never longed for the gift of speaking in tongues

and felt uncomfortable when someone else had the gift, now it was flowing out of my mouth regardless of my will. I prayed as my mouth moved reluctantly. The Holy Spirit fell on me more and more as I prayed in tongues. Time went by, and the young people had gone home, and the church was empty. I was excited by having a spiritual experience, but on the one hand, I was worried about what others might have thought of me.

The assistant pastor who lived next to the church came to me with his wife when I was about to leave. They smiled as if they have witnessed everything and said it is clear that I received the gift of tongues. The assistant pastor explained that God's power is not limited to speaking in tongues, but that there are many different kinds of gifts that can be also passed on to others. In my third year of undergraduate studies, at the age of 26, I formally stepped into the spiritual world. As I listened to the assistant pastor, many critics for the gifts of the Holy Spirit, and my vigilance against the spiritual world weakened.

Immerse in the Bible
I prayed hard in my undergraduate days and was into reading the word of God. When I did not go to school or was on vacation, I read the Bible all day. It was popular to draw lines with various colored pens when reading books at the time. I also read the Bible underlining with different colored pens depending on the content. For example, I used blue for spiritual content, red for words of blessing, and yellow for words of curse.

I read 70 to 100 pages of the Bible a day. Reading at this rate, I could read the Bible twice a month. God's words were literally like honey in my mouth. In the Bible class, the professor checked how much the students read the Bible, and I always aimed for the first place. In my newlywed days when we had no children, I do not remember going on a travel, watching a movie, or shopping with my wife. Having had such an uninteresting husband, my wife probably had not enjoyed the newlywed life. Anyway, it was so rewarding and fun to study theology for me to become a pastor.

Hear the Voice of God

I was filled with the Holy Spirit every day at 27 years old, and the department I was in charge of was also full of God's grace. I always yearned for God with my heart. When I fell asleep while reading the Bible, it appeared in my dreams, and sometimes its pages went over in my dreams. The text of the Bible and the number of pages were also precisely noticeable, which was a fantastic experience. On Sunday, sometimes, I preached with the text that God showed me in a dream. When it happened, it was effortless to set the sermon text for the week. I hoped that God would teach me what to preach every week in this way.

On the day I heard God's voice, I fell asleep reading the Bible all day long. During my sleep, at some point, my mind became clear. Then my body began to harden slowly. The moment I thought, 'What's going on?' my body became completely stiff. I tried to move, but I could not move a bit. The fear flowed over that I was having some kinds of serious health issues. I could not move a finger or a toe. I tried to open my mouth and speak, but my mouth would not open, and my voice would not come out. I was completely paralyzed.

To get out of this crisis, I tried to call for help from my wife, who was sleeping beside me, but I could not get my message across. I was utterly alone revealed in danger. Then a mysterious vision appeared in reality, not in a dream. I can not say for sure whether it was my soul or my unconsciousness, but I had a feeling of seeing above the sky. Then came the voice "PRIEST" from high above. I certainly heard these six alphabets clearly, which sounded like God speaking to Moses in the movie, *The Ten Commandments*. It was an authoritative and loud voice. I heard the voice of God as my whole body was immersed in God's presence. Emotions such as fear, trembling, and awe that can not be expressed in words were felt all at once; I was completely lost in this mystery.

As soon as God stopped speaking, my body naturally returned to a normal state, and I was able to escape from fear. I got up and looked up the word priest in the English dictionary, and found out that it meant a priest. I also looked for any other possible meanings; however, I was convinced that God had called me as a priest that night. "Yes. I am a priest."

I did not wake my wife, but quietly knelt and prayed for hours. I was sure that God had appeared and spoken to me. It was twelve years ago that I was bitten by a serpent and promised to be his servant on the verge of death, and ten years ago that I experienced a profound conversion. About a decade later, God visited me to call me as his servant. It is not difficult to find people who experienced such spiritual calling in church history.

After this mysterious spiritual experience, I felt as if I was walking on a cloud. I read the Bible, served the church, and studied harder than before. I had no time to hang out with my friends. I went to the theater only once with my classmate while attending the seminary for seven years. Spending time outdoors with friends can be counted on the fingers of one hand. I was so after God that I had never had coffee with a female student in my school days.

When I shared my experience of God with my close friends, few believed me. Most of them sarcastically asked back, "Are you a mystic?" I was so happy to encounter God, but people treated me like a sinner. Even at a very spiritual prayer meeting, they did not acknowledge my experience. My heart was on fire, but the eyes around me were cold.

After I had a spiritual experience, my desire to know God became greater. I visited several professors because I was zealous to know more about spiritual gifts, but their answers were not satisfactory to my heart. Yet, professor Young-Bae Cha had an open-mind on the spiritual gifts, so he guided me personally several times. He used Herman Bavinck's *Our Reasonable Faith* as teaching material in the class, and I found this book very helpful. I still love the writings of Bavinck.

I had a desire to confirm my experience in church history. So I bought and read the writings of Sundar Singh, Emanuel Swedenborg, St. Augustine, and St. Francis at the bookstore. Going through the books of monks and those who pursued spirituality, I was convinced that my experience was not problematic, either biblically or historically. It could have been a little different from the theological ideas I was learning. However, even though theology changes, the words of God and the experiences of saints do not change.

The spiritual experience of hearing God's voice became a significant boost in my ministry throughout life. When things went well, I always tried to be humble and conscious of the living God, and when things went bad, I could endure hardship and serve God not giving up since I had the conviction that God had called me as a priest.

No matter how hard and difficult the ministry was, I had never thought of having another job. My lifelong wish is to live according to God-given vocation until my last breath. Also, I will greatly welcome if my children dedicate themselves to work for the kingdom of God.

After encountering God, I realized that this world was not so important. From then on, I lost my greed for this world. The only thing that mattered was "how I will stand before God in the end."

After 25 years of experiencing God's presence, I asked the world-wide spiritual ministers when I had chances to meet them, whether my experience was real or not, and if it is real, which among the trinity had spoken to me that night. I will not reveal their names, but they all envied me, saying that the Father God himself had appeared. Some of them said they never had this kind of experience. They also said that meeting the Father God is not common even in the Bible and that only a handful of people experienced him in church history. Only a few people have ever experienced a heavenly father while on the earth since the creation.

Not everyone can experience God as I have experienced him. And not all of us must have the same spiritual experience as others. It was not my intention to encounter God in such a way; it was God's intention. A pure and deeper level of spiritual experience almost all the time begins first with God.

Praise in tongues

I learned negative theological theories about the gift of the Holy Spirit in the seminary, but my longing for the spiritual gifts was not quenched. I remember the humor that a chaplain said in his sermon when I first entered the seminary. "During the first year of study, students' hearts are on fire. But on the way, their hearts cool down, and only smoke arises, by the time they graduate; they become cold-hearted." He probably wanted to emphasize that theological education is biased toward theory and neglects both spiritual and experiential sides.

I do not know about others, but I was not the case. I received grace at every Chapel hour and prepared as a good pastor. I was able to speak in tongues, but because of the conservative school atmosphere, I did not speak in tongues and did not talk much about the gift of the Holy Spirit to avoid being bullied. But my heart overflowed with grace.

One evening it rained a lot on the way home from worship. I walked for about ten minutes in the rain because I forgot to bring an umbrella. There were few people on the road, perhaps because it was night. As I walked in the rain, my feet were immersed in water; at the same time, I was also immersed in grace. And hymns in tongues flowed out of my mouth. No one was listening, but I was not conscious of my surroundings. I sang praise as the sound came out of me. Hymns flowed unceasingly in a beautiful language. It was mainly a high-pitched one. I thought, 'Angels would sing this way.' However, I did not praise in tongues in front of my family, fellow pastors, and saints because I wanted to avoid unnecessary misunderstanding and prejudice.

After many years, when my spiritual vision was opened, praising in tongues was also restored. Now, I can sing spiritual songs more elegantly and more in-depth. My heart trembles when I praise in tongues. It sounds beautiful and spiritual. Spiritual saints like spiritual songs very much, and some are even thrilled. I like to praise in tongues when I am alone since it satisfies my soul and leads me closer to the Lord.

CHAPTER 9

CRY OUT FOR REPENTANCE AND HOLINESS

I was interested in pneumatology because my parents ministered with many spiritual gifts, and I had many spiritual experiences and gifts as well. I bought and read countless books dealing with pneumatology. Among other books, I realized one basic spiritual principle from reading R. A. Torrey's *The Holy Spirit:* repentance is the most critical factor to receive the Holy Spirit. If there are many sins, it is difficult for the Holy Spirit to work.

Since I longed for the Holy Spirit, even though I have not repented thoroughly as I am now, I was always cautious not to sin and prayed over my sins. I easily became emotional when praying, repenting, and preaching.

I cried a lot listening to the sermon during the chapel. Sometimes I cried too much that I was not in a condition to go to lunch. Other students and professors frequently criticized preachings rationally, but I was touched by most of the sermons, and my heart was on fire when I heard them.

One day, I went to a summer retreat with the youth group I was pastoring. Senior pastor entrusted me with over 50 college students; I had to lead them by myself. I delivered the message in the morning and evening. From the first day of the retreat, I encouraged students to repent strongly as John the Baptist cried out for repentance. That evening we had a time of intense repentance, and one by one, we got up and confessed our sins. This was the method used by Pastor Yoon-Sun Park, and I led the prayer meeting in the same way. One person repented of riding the bus for a student fare, even though he was not a student. Another person repented that he had dated too many women.

The cries of repentance burst here and there. Our youth department was full of vitality and grew day by day. The secret to gain spiritual sight lies in repentance. I have invested a tremendous amount of time in repentance. The truth that never changes is that when a man repents, God gives grace. Church history proves that the Welsh Revival Movement in England in 1906 and the Pyongyang Great Revival Movement in 1907 began with repentance.

Decide to Live for the Lowly

It was rewarding and enjoyable to serve the church as an educational evangelist while studying at the seminary. It was better to serve, teach, or preach in the church than to study only. Just as having a solid theological background is critical in serving God, it is also crucial to have spirituality. Yet, most people put much energy on only one side, which is usually the former one. Anyway, because I devoted my life to God's kingdom, I wanted to do my best for God in everything I do.

When I was in my late twenties, people thought I did not suffer much. I thought I had a lot of troubles, but people's evaluations were quite different from mine. Of course, I have never starved, or

I never took a leave of absence because of tuition while studying at the graduate and undergraduate school. In this respect, indeed, I did not suffer much.

Somehow, I always felt that I should be in a ministry for the poor and the sick. I mentioned this to my youth group many times. On the other hand, however, the desire to establish a big church in Seoul began to take place in my heart little by little.

By the time I graduated from the seminary, there was a bit of anxiety in my mind. I had a lot of thoughts about where and how to do the ministry, so I spent a lot of time praying on this matter. In the meantime, the pastor of the rural church supported by our church resigned. As soon as I heard the news I volunteered to go.

I explained to my pastor that I was not at ease living as I am now; I have lived and studied in Seoul mostly without a big hardship. He replied that he would discuss the matter with the elders. I returned home and got my wife's consent. A week later, however, the pastor said, elders disagreed with sending me to the countryside because I was serving the church at the moment. I think the elders thought it was better for the church that I stay. My swollen dream has withered like that. Nevertheless, I wanted to leave Seoul and go to the province. I believed that was what I had to do for God.

Once again, an opportunity came to me. A church in Seongnam was looking for a full-time evangelist. I applied and joined the church. In the previous church, about 550 people attended Sunday service, but this church only had 200 members. Compared to the previous church, there were a lot of deficiencies in many ways. Frankly speaking, I wanted to work in a more challenging and smaller church setting than this, but God trained me here.

CHAPTER 10

ENCOUNTER EVIL SPIRITS

While studying at the graduate school of theology, I served the primary department in the newly appointed church. Before summer bible camp, I went to a prayer house near Dobong mountain to hold a prayer meeting with teachers from other departments. About 30 kindergarten and elementary school teachers sat on the rock and prayed. A young man approached us and interrupted our prayers; he yelled and swore at us as he passed by. He seemed to be demon-possessed.

There were several spiritual people among the teachers. One of them came up to me and asked, "Why don't we drive a demon out of him?" Some teachers agreed. Those who prayed together were mostly deacons and deaconess who were at least ten years older than me. At the time, I was not even thirty years old, so I could not disagree when they suggested to cast out evil spirits. On the one hand, I was grateful that they believed I could take the lead in driving out evil spirits.

We stopped praying and caught the man in our way. I told him that he needs prayer, and we want to pray for him. Contrary to our expectations, he readily accepted our proposal. About ten people continued to pray for the summer camp, while the other ten rented a room in a prayer house and began praying for him. I have never had any previous experience of treating a demon-possessed person. Yet I thought to myself, 'What's the big deal? If the people of God pray, the evil spirits will go out.'

We prayed aloud, and we shouted out evil spirits to come out of him. After a while, the man began to react. So far, he has kept saying strange things to us, but he lost his strength and became quiet. Then a bubble came out of his mouth. The atmosphere was hotting up because we felt that evil spirits were coming out of his body.

We could not see evil spirits leaving, nor did we know what will happen if they leave his body completely. However, many people drove out demons in the Bible, and I witnessed my father driving out demons many times, so I thought I could do it too. Above all, we could take courage because we were praying people.

We prayed for him for three hours. The bubbles came out of his mouth, but somehow it did not seem that he was getting better. He sometimes said, "I'm going out" or other strange words that were hard to understand. It was hard to say that he had significantly improved compared to his initial state. As dawn approached, we, who had to attend the dawn prayer, began to be impatient. We looked at a watch and gave each other a sign of what to do with the situation. The demon-possessed man talking in nonsense suddenly said, "It's time for you guys to go down right?" I was horrified and drained of energy the moment I heard him.

The evil spirits in him was seeing through our situation. When we prayed against the evil spirits, they were struck a little but did not leave him. The demons that were staying in him were stronger than ours; therefore, we could not cast them out with our power. We came down from the mountain after hours of unfulfilled prayer. I kept this incident on my mind for a long time and lamented my incompetence. My mother also said it was a pity. I learned that not everyone can drive out evil spirits.

Attack by Demons

As the probationer exam was just around the corner, my senior pastor gave me a week off to study. I stayed and studied at a prayer house in Gwangju, Gyeonggi-do. The facilities here were not excellent. There were several small lodgings, and the first room was a single room. I prayed and studied alone in that room.

One rainy evening, there were only a few people in the prayer house besides me. After studying for hours, I was tired, so I lied down for a while, facing the door. And then a strange thing happened. I was looking at the door with my eyes open, and suddenly two goblins slid into the room without opening the door. They had two horns, round eyes, and black bodies. When they smiled at me, their white teeth came out.

One of them sat on my neck, and the other sat on my chest while I was thinking, 'What are they?' not grasping the situation. The goblins laughed, looking at my face, and my body was paralyzed in a moment.

Five years ago, I was paralyzed under the presence of God, but now I was paralyzed by demons sitting on my body. I could not move a finger; I was completely paralyzed. The bigger problem was that I could not breathe because of the goblin sitting on my chest.

After two minutes, I felt like dying because I could not breathe. I was dumbfounded at the thought that I might die in this way. It did not make sense because I did not fulfill my calling yet. For nearly 20 years, I have lived to become God's servant; therefore, dying like this was nonsense.

No matter how much I wanted to shout "In the name of Jesus of Nazareth," I was choked out. I tried to speak against them, but my mouth would not open, and my voice would not come out. I was heartbroken thinking, 'I'm really going to die.' But as time passed, my neck was released slightly, and I was able to breathe a little.

As chance came, I squeezed my voice and said, "Go away, you evil spirits." Then the hands of a goblin gripping my throat loosened a bit, and both of them got up at the same time and went a step backward from me. I shouted a little louder again, "Jesus of Nazareth!" Then the goblins turned around and escaped through the closed door.

As soon as they stood up, my senses came back. I sprang to my feet, opened the door, and followed the goblins. "Where are these things?" I yelled and looked around, but I could not find them. It was dark outside, and it was drizzling. I came back to my room and wept loudly because my pride was hurt so badly.

I was so ashamed at the fact that I was attacked by Satan and could not resist. I met the father God; my earthly father was the head of the prayer house; I learned theology from great professors; I was about to become a minister. These facts made me more unbearable.

From then on, I always mention two things when I talk about spiritual experiences: an exciting story of experiencing God's presence and hearing his voice, and a shameful story of nearly being killed, attacked by Satan. For decades, only a few had believed my story.

CHAPTER 11

START A PASTORAL MINISTRY

Plant a Church and God's Provision

I have ordained a pastor at 33 years old. It has been 18 years since I determined to become a pastor. I could not open my eyes properly because hot tears rolled down my face. When I looked back on myself to see if I was well prepared as God's servant, I could not be satisfied. I was ashamed when I saw myself lacking and full of faults. Despite my shortcoming, I became a pastor because it was my only goal.

I started a church, but I had nothing in hand. Since God has led me so far, I trusted the Lord's guidance and provision. At first, several saints supplied the necessary materials. I still remember one of them. There was a sister, who had just registered to the church; she served the Lord with a great deal of material. Soon afterward, she got married and ran a supermarket by herself. She brought all the groceries and household items for our family.

We were provided with much of the daily necessities through her. Since our couple was pastoring without the help of others, we felt more grateful for the sister's help. When we thanked her sincerely, she replied, "God told me to help you." Her answer made me think about a lot of things. She also said, "I started a supermarket because I wanted to fill your needs."

I was confused by what she said. I could not discern whether God really said this to her, or she was obsessed with a strange spirit or if it was her own thoughts. The person who provided daily necessities heard the voice of God, but I, a recipient, heard nothing. I was annoyed every day because of this, but God did not say anything.

Sometimes when I felt her help was too much, I refused to receive it. Yet, she continued to bring us what we needed. Once I visited the supermarket, and there were more items piled up in my house than in the store. I asked myself, 'Is this normal?' Nevertheless, her service lasted for more than a year, and it was of great help to our couple who had just begun the ministry.

See a Vision of Other Church

My close friend was pastoring near our church. I visited his church about once or twice a year. His church was growing little by little, and I had the church in my mind.

One night I saw my friend's church in a dream. A red serpent was coiling around the cross of the church steeple. I was amazed and woke up from my dream, but I did not share what I saw.

I could not tell for sure what the dream meant, but it was certainly an ominous sign. After a while, my friend left the church which was growing, and the church disappeared after being integrated with another church. Many of the saints who attended the church moved away or moved to another church.

As time went by, I became convinced that God had shown me what will happen in the future. Pastoring itself, in the first place, is a matter of making people believe in an invisible God and fighting against an invisible Satan. Therefore, spiritual activities related to spiritual battles can happen anytime.

Since I had experienced many spiritual phenomena, I did not doubt that the vision I saw in a dream was from God. All the spiritual experiences of individuals may not have come from God. Yet, I believe that we should acknowledge the spiritual experiences of others who have borne many fruits in their lives.

Resign from the Church

By the time I was in my late 30s, I had about 80 members. Due to a small problem, some left the church, and about 60 people remained. Since most of our church members were older than me, it was a challenging environment to pastor without spiritual authority. But going through many things, my authority was weakened.

One week during the daytime service, a young woman in her thirties came to me with a look of embarrassment as soon as the service was over: "I'm in trouble, reverend." I usually greeted every member and had a lot of things to do right after the service, but she held on to me and said over and over again, not caring about the others. I listened to her, wondering what had happened.

I had never been to her house, nor her husband attended our church, nor did I know much about the lady since she had no position in the church. I was aware of her just as an educated and classy woman. Out of nowhere, she said, "My husband said that you are going to resign from the church, you can't do that, please don't resign." With a tearful look on her face, she dissuaded me from resigning.

She shared about her family and husband, perhaps because I did not seem to believe in her words. They originally lived in the

Gangnam area, which is the southern part of the Han river but recently moved to our neighborhood. She said her husband is a pastor who prays a lot, adding that he is a very spiritual person.

According to her, her husband, who has never seen my face, said a few days ago that "Your pastor will soon resign and leave the church." Because she trusted her husband, she said, "I'm sure you are resigning." I could not just ignore the words since she was a sophisticated and elegant person, but it was such an absurd remark. I replied with a smile, "That's never going to happen. Even if the ministry is a bit difficult now, I've never thought of resigning." This is how our conversation ended.

I smiled whenever I remembered her words. A week after the conversation, I have done some legwork to get an office, for I was planning to organize a mission with few friends, apart from pastoral ministry.

I was able to push ahead with my work with a lively mind without any worries because I was promised a large sum of money to get an office by someone. I made a list of what I had to do as the president of the mission. I was busy for a week and then came to the weekend.

I met a deaconess who promised to sponsor the mission on Saturday. In the course of solving a problem that occurred not long ago concerning another church, she saw me addressing the issue wisely and valued me. Since I knew that, I could ask her to support the mission I was about to organize.

The deaconess had leadership along with economic power. She was eager to help me because she was impressed at my enthusiasm to run a mission with great aspirations. But she made me an unexpected suggestion. She did not just want to support me by material but offered to work together. Her husband, an elder, owned a large corporation; they had a lot of land and a large fortune.

She had already established a mission-based church, and about 150 members attended Sunday service. She told me that if I decide to take charge of the church, she can help grow it into the largest church in the Gangbuk area, a northern part of the Han river. She also added she can serve the church with great wealth and has a considerable amount of land right next to the big street.

Frankly speaking, it is not easy for a pastor serving size of about 70 members to refuse such an offer on the spot. It was my lifelong dream to become a pastor and a true shepherd. I desired to be a genuine pastor, not just a pastor in charge of a big church. I was grateful that she had made this proposal in recognition of me, and I was glad to see a way to carry out my big pastoral dream.

After much consideration, I replied that I will resign from the mission I was going to establish and the church I was serving and accept her offer. However, before leaving the church which I founded, I told her that there are few things to be solved first. But she spoke strongly that it is God's will to resign the church tomorrow and work with her from the day after tomorrow.

It was impossible. When a senior pastor leaves the church, there is a lot of work to be done, and problems are bound to arise. I was well aware of this fact, but she urged me to make a decision quickly. I replied that I would think positively and came back home. My heart sank when I remembered what the lady said last Sunday.

I was so puzzled because I did not hear anything from God, while a man who did not even know me heard God's voice about my resignation and another woman so convinced that it is God's will to resign right away. "Am I God's servant? Am I a spiritual leader?" I wanted to be a good pastor, but in reality, I was a spiritually dull man. "Why am I the only one who doesn't know God's will?" I returned home with a confused mind.

When I was agonizing over the matter, something happened that made me decide to resign. My wife informed me that several deacons gathered to talk about church problems. I was a self-respecting man and was still in high spirits, so it was not acceptable that they had gathered without me.

That evening I stayed up all night praying on the pulpit. My conclusion was to tender my resignation. I did not hear God's voice or his response but decided to believe what others said. How can I disobey God's will? When they insist it is God's will. I could not figure out the aftermath, but I submitted my resignation after the Sunday service. Congregations were tremendously confused, and I was criticized severely. Some of them extremely dissuaded me from leaving. Leaving all this behind, I preached at a new church from the following week.

Pray Earnestly in a New Church

The new church provided me a nice house and a car. They also gave me a driver insisting that I should not drive myself. I visited many homes of our members in that car. Most church members were young; the church was rich, and nothing lacked. I accepted most of the suggestions of the deaconess who led me here.

After a few months, she proposed to start all-night prayer meetings for 40 days. At night, I prayed with 20 to 30 church leaders, and at dawn, I led the dawn prayer meeting. If God did not allow me strength, it was impossible to carry out all the schedules. Thankfully, God gave me energy, and I was able to handle heavy schedules.

Not so long after we had finished prayer meetings, the

deaconess proposed to pray for 40 days again for the church this time. She said I do not have to if I do not want to, but her determined attitude showed that the remark was empty.

I had to pray for another 40 nights against my will. I prayed all night, took a nap for a while, and went to church again to lead the dawn prayer gathering. During the day, I had to visit many homes of church members. I can not remember having a whole day off. The church I first started had material difficulties, but I was not overwhelmed by church works. Now, we were abundant, but I had a little free time. I was out of my mind working day and night. I received hard training unexpectedly. If ministry was something that I had to move on to such a tight schedule, I was not sure how much further I could do it. I led 40 days night prayer meeting three times a year.

Then one night, a man came into the church carrying a woman in her 40s on his back when bout 20 church leaders gathered to pray. When I asked him what was going on, he said, "I think she's demon-possessed. I thought about taking her to the hospital, but I changed my mind and took her to the church." He already visited several churches, but they were all closed. When he was wondering what to do, he saw a light coming out of our church. He pleaded with me to cast out demons in this woman.

I asked how he knew this woman, and he said he is a customer of her liquor shop. He was having a cup of tea with her, and suddenly she fell, making a strange noise. He felt responsible because he was a Christian and came into our church to help her somehow.

He did not want his identity to be revealed, so he left the woman to us. I have never healed a demon-possessed person before, so I was very disconcerted. As mentioned earlier, I tried to drive out demons with several others about ten years ago, but it did not work. Since then, I have never reencountered this kind of situation. The thought of 'What if I fail again?' crossed my mind. I was an evangelist when I failed, but I was a senior pastor this time. In other words, I had more to lose. A courageous evangelist and deaconess wanted to pray for her, so the church leaders and I began to pray together for the lady.

We laid her down, sat around her, and prayed. When we finished praying, the woman evangelist made her pray through the Lord's Prayer. She had never been to church but read the Lord's Prayer on the page in front of the hymn several times, blinking her eyes. She twisted herself and was very distressed, but she followed our guidance well. Some of us went home in fear, but nearly 20 people prayed fervently. By the time the sun rose, she almost came back to her senses, and we cheered.

The lady said whenever she felt lonely at the bar, she often went to a famous temple behind Dobong Mountain. She confessed that when she was drinking with a deacon last night, she began to talk nonsense and twisted her body unconsciously.

The lady did not know Jesus, but she expressed her gratitude for being healed. I had a hard time praying all night, but I was very excited to heal a demon-possessed person for the first time in my life. We introduced the woman to a prayer house we knew well and advised her to receive more prayers there because I was too busy with my pastoral schedule to spare time for this woman. After a week, she visited our church to say thank-you because she was healed completely.

As the end of the year approached, we had many meetings over the administration of the church for the next year. There was some disagreement between the elder and me. When I think about it now, it was not a big deal, but it came as a big burden to me as a young pastor at the time. There was some noise in our church that could be in any church. However, it did not matter much because any church can have small problems.

I made a significant decision while having a conversation with the deaconess who invited me to the church. She told me, "There is a man of God who prays a lot, and he said that you are serving our church only temporarily." The deaconess was a very spiritual person and feared God. She had a mentor, the head of prayer house, who gave spiritual advice whenever a critical event came up. The deaconess always obeyed the mentor because she considered his words as the words of God.

Since the head of the prayer house, whom the deaconess respected and followed, said I was just a pastor who serves church only for a while, I had no reason to stay anymore. I also feared God, and I obeyed God's will all the time. The reason she called me to work together was also because of his advice.

I did not want to ruin God's plan or will because of my benefits and interests. I just hoped that the spiritual director's words were right, and even if they were not true, the deaconess who trusted his words became a major obstacle. I felt uncomfortable serving the church too. So I resigned in a few weeks, without any countermeasures, despite the dissuasion around me. Many people debated why I was leaving, but the biggest reason was that I feared God. People of God, of all ages, do not cling to their positions. This world, especially the church, is in God's hands. The only thing I regretted was that I did not know the will of God directly again this time.

CHAPTER 12

WORK AT THE PRAYER HOUSE

I was able to resign easily because I had something to count on. My father ran a local prayer house for ten years. Since he was nearly seventy years old, someone had to succeed him. My father never asked me to take over the prayer house, but my mother offered me many times. She wanted me to come down to where they are and do ministry together. My mother was a woman of prayer; thus, I believed that she knew God's will, so I considered her request seriously. Also, I had some confidence to work at the prayer house since I turned 40 years old and involved in pastoral ministry for five years now.

Shortly after I resigned from the church, I went to the prayer house where my father was and became the vice-president. My father led the early morning service, and I led the evening service. Also, I did a lot of labors because the church building was under remodeling. We also built new accommodation. I made a large space for visitors to exercise, and I even planted trees here and there. And I paved the road with concrete because the road to our prayer house was unpaved.

We tried not to hire workers for all these works. The whole

family worked together most of the time. I hardly ever labored before, nor had any related talents. It was amazing that I got involved in architecture and civil engineering every day. In church history, monks made labor essential with prayer. Now that I have started a prayer house, I made up my mind to labor like monks. More people visited our prayer center when I was there for nearly a year, and it became lively.

I went up to Seoul once a week because I gave a lecture at a small seminary. Occasionally, I was asked to lead a revival meeting too. When I was pastoring, not many people considered me spiritually, but strangely after I came here, many people saw me as a spiritually competent person. Many people came to me to discuss important matters. Because I had no spiritual ability that people expected, I felt a great burden every time I had to consult people. Quite a lot of people came to our center for counseling, although they had spiritual leaders at their churches.

Most visitors were from Seoul, and they were well educated from a prominent university. Famous figures who were hard to meet in the church also visited the prayer house frequently. They treated me like a great man, which I felt very uncomfortable. Since these people all had their pastors in Seoul, as a pastor myself, I had to consider their pastors' positions.

If our church members had gone to another prayer house to discuss their important issues with other spiritual leaders, I would have felt incompetent. In connection with this, it reminded me why I resigned from my previous church. It was due to the deaconess who respected the head of the prayer center too much. It was all because of his words that I left the church and am now working hard here.

I was worried that those who trusted and followed the words

of someone other than their pastors would be misled and harmed. I also felt uneasy with people who said, "This is the will of God or that is the will of God." Perhaps because I was not very spiritual enough to know God's will. I was always curious about how people knew God's will, and I doubted all the time if it was true. Regardless of my conflict, I was now in a position where I had to solve the spiritual problems of others.

From time to time, my heart was saddened at the thought that I may have to do only this kind of ministry for the rest of my life. Whenever this thought came across my mind, I was discouraged because my dream was to have a wonderful pastoral ministry in a decent place in Seoul. I grew up in Seoul, so I was most familiar with Seoul. I believed that doing a ministry at a place where I knew best would probably bear most fruits.

Sometimes I thought about going abroad to study. At the time, many of my seminary friends went abroad to study or returned from studying abroad. My classmates occasionally asked me, "What are you doing these days?" This question bothered me all the time. To speak honestly, I did not have the ability or material to study abroad; it was just my greed to study overseas. And I faced an incident that neatly laid out my desire to study more.

A deacon from Seoul stayed at our center and prayed for weeks. He graduated from one of the top universities in Korea, earned a doctorate in engineering from an American university, and served as a researcher at a famous research institute in the United States. He was scouted as a professional executive and was the CEO of a company in Seoul. He told me that I do not need to study further since I graduated from Hapdong Theological Seminary. It was very unexpected to hear that from someone who studied so much.

When I was at Shinsung Church a decade ago, the president

of the youth group, who graduated from a prestigious university and was a researcher at KAIST, also said, "Education is not the most important qualification to the Lord's servant."

When the deacon said I do not have to study further, he implied that the Lord's servant should build more spirituality. He told me another story of someone he knew. When he was in the State, a person who only had a master's degree became the had of an institution and instructed hundreds of researchers with doctoral degrees. By telling this story, he wanted to say that I can do great things regardless of my academic background if I build up my spiritual ability. In that sense, he encouraged me that my experiences at this prayer center will serve as a stepping stone later in my ministry. I still live on his exhortation. Knowledge is essential, but the most important thing for the ministers is to have spiritual power. When it comes to spiritual power, it covers so many things, such as an ability to talk with God. Ever since I was encouraged by his words, I was able to stand tall in front of friends who had doctoral degrees.

Yet, I had no intention to stay here forever. I was not spiritually prepared to serve at the prayer center, nor was labor fit to my grain. I was not fit for this ministry in many ways. Also, my parents' lives disappointed me. Although they ministered with spiritual gifts, their lives did not meet my expectation. I had a high standard that people with special gifts should be holy, gracious, and mature because they received great grace of God, but that was not my parents' life.

I had some conflicts with my father while I had these discomforts in my heart, so I seriously discussed with my mother whether I should go back to Seoul and do a pastoral ministry or stay here and continue this ministry.

My mother advised me to go to Seoul. I took her opinion

because I could not hear God's voice, no matter how hard I prayed. I trusted her advice as God's will because she prayed a lot. I came to the prayer house following my mother's advice, and I also followed my mother's opinion when I left the prayer house. I had no choice but to rely on others in spiritual matters.

In addition, influential pastors and saints who visited our center often said that it was a waste to spend the years at the prayer center for someone young and competent like me. Their words also moved me. After briefly discussing with my wife, I came up to Seoul a few days later, without making any arrangements. My wife and children stayed at the prayer house for a few more months and then came to Seoul.

CHAPTER 13

SPIRITUAL TRANSITION

Disappoint with Saints

During eight years of pastoring, I was disappointed with saints and God. I always wished to become a pastor since young and lived only for him. Yet it seemed that he was not with me and was not willing to bless me. I turned forty, but I could not find many fruits in my ministry in the standards of others and spiritually.

I newly planted a church, and about 50 people gathered; however, their faith was weak, and their behaviors were immature. The situation was not much different from the previous churches. The hardest part in pastoring for me was when saints depended on me instead of relying on God, and they were too conscious of each other. As children of God, we must serve God with pure heart, yet most people worked to receive praise or attention from pastors or other church members. This was true not only of new believers but also of people who had the faith for years. Since young, I have focused on God more than anything else, so it was challenging for me to get along with saints who leaned on me.

There were many relational problems in the church that would not have happened if saints looked to God. I was gradually disappointed with the congregation. I was told, "This is what pastoral ministry is originally about," and I was also advised that "It is wise to curry favor with the congregation." But I began to question from deep in my heart, 'What is pastoring?' I had to find the answer to this question in order to move forward, so I pondered upon it many days and had to decide how and by what standards I should minister. I was not sure if the ministry that other pastors advised me was the one that God expected from me. Nevertheless, I could not come up with a definite answer: "This is what pastoral ministry is!" or "This is how true shepherd supposed to look like!"

On one occasion, we invited a speaker to our church to hold a revival meeting. He asked people to come out in line if they want to receive the gift of tongues. I was amazed to witness many saints going out and lining up. They tried to speak in tongues as the speaker instructed, which was not real. Although I belonged to the conservative denomination, I admitted the gift of speaking in tongues because I also had the experience. However, I taught my congregations that speaking in tongues is not something special, nor did I encourage them to pray in tongues. But the congregation had a longing for spiritual gifts and spiritual experiences in their hearts, to the extent that several years of my teachings were overshadowed; speaking in tongues was only one of their desire.

I did my best to follow the guidelines of the denomination to which I belonged, yet it was revealed that the spiritual needs of my flock and doctrines were contrary to each other. I could not figure out a way to fill in this gap. Throughout the ministry, this issue collided. I lost balance and the principle of ministry. I was proficient in the Bible and theology, but I was unsure how to guide my flock and lost the way.

SPIRITUAL TRANSITION

I spent a lot of time on the activities outside the church for nearly five to six years from the mid-forties. I visited foreign countries several times, worked hard at presbytery, and handled several tasks at the general assembly. Also, I felt rewarded, working for the seminary alumni association.

I participated in various religious gatherings such as the Korean Pastoral Association and socialized with leading pastors. Perhaps I put more energy into this than pastoral care because I wanted to have a fellowship with pastors whose level of spirituality was higher than the childlike saints. Once I stepped into external activities, I could not easily quit. Perhaps I have gained great satisfaction, whether spiritual or physical, through external activities.

On the other hand, the church I was in charge of was stagnant. Yet I was not burdened or bothered because I was disappointed with the saints and God anyway. Perhaps that was the reason why I was not so enthusiastic about going to a little larger church when they were interested in me. At that time, I was deeply hurt by the ministry. In a way, I was just wasting my time.

A Young Man with Unclean Spirit

Meanwhile, I confronted another incident that made me disappointed in myself again. I got a call from a deaconess when I was taking a rest. She told me that a young man in the church was possessed by a demon and was acting strangely, so I rushed to the church.

As I stepped into the church, I witnessed a scene that was so embarrassing: the young man was walking around the church naked. Not only was he tall and handsome, but he was also preparing for the state examination as a senior in a prestigious university. His incomprehensible behavior was a shocking event to me as well as to his family.

I asked him to come to his senses and get dressed quickly, but he refused to listen. The bigger problem was that the younger brother, who came to stop him, began to gibberish like him. I did not know what to do. The problem did not stop here but became more serious. The brother's father, too, a deacon, soon began to gibberish like his two sons. Three men, the father, and two sons walked around the church in spiritual darkness.

I felt helpless because there was nothing I could do as a pastor. A pastor should be able to solve the problems of his congregation, especially when it comes to the spiritual ones. However, I felt so pathetic that I could not solve the problem of the saints and that I could not treat or help them when they were sick. In fact, I should have prevented this in advance as a spiritual leader before it arose to the surface.

I literally did not know what to do, but I took his younger brother, who was relatively fine, into a room and laid him down. He followed my instruction well and stayed still when I prayed for him. Then, I used all the methods I could, such as praying, convincing, and a bit of force, to make this young man dress up again.

The next day, their father called me and asked me to come to his house quickly, so I rushed to the house at a dash. The brother who caused trouble yesterday was in a bad state again. This time he was baptizing his father with water. I scolded him for his behavior, but shockingly he insisted that he was God. I rebuked him, but this time, he began to say weird things, revealing his parents' sins and faults. Whether they were true or not, he was shaming the whole family.

I lost my words to see such a wonderful young man with good

faith being caught by Satan and doing what Satan told him. I was too ashamed to stand before God and saints; I had neither the ability to cast out demons nor to cure people. So after discussing with his parents, we decided to send him to the prayer house they knew well, and I took him there and came back home.

I heard this and that from a saint the next day. The couple was very disappointed with me yesterday. They used to attend a big church but moved to this neighborhood to send their son to a seminary. After visiting many churches, they chose our church because they thought I was the most spiritual and gifted minister; however, I failed to meet their expectation.

This couple hoped that their pastor would solve their spiritual problems. I can not say that their expectation or attitude is wrong, for it is natural for the flock to depend on the shepherd. Perhaps I should have made an offer to treat their son first. Therefore, I had nothing to say to them, although they were disappointed with me.

There were many twists and turns before the whole family recovered from their spiritual darkness by God's grace, but thankfully, they all overcame. There was not a percent of my credit in this work. Whenever I was reminded of this family, I blamed myself for my incompetence as a minister; I was not even a pastor!

A Message from a Saint

After ten years of ministry, I turned fifty. I have always had the idea of staying at one church for at least a decade, whether I was doing good or not. I had come to a crossroads of choosing whether to keep on the ordinary ministry or turn in a different direction.

When I was still young, I was filled with the Holy Spirit and met both God and demons. But now, I no longer experienced any kind of spiritual phenomenon. My reality as a pastor seemed miserable. However, even if I had spiritual gifts since my denomination was very conservative, it would certainly not have been easy to partake in the spiritual ministry.

My name was well known in my denomination since I have put my time and energy into outside activities over the past decade. For this reason, I had no courage to be criticized by my acquaintances for pursuing spiritual ministry. Of course, there was no guarantee that my spirituality would recover and that spiritual gifts would appear strongly to me just because I seek spirituality; I was in a dilemma.

One day, an acquaintance came to see me saying she has something important to share. She was a person I knew from ten years ago when I worked at a prayer house, and she had a good relationship with my parents too. She believed that I had considerable spiritual ability. That is why she attended our Sunday service several times.

She said, "God will use you the greatest in the Far East region." Then, she proposed to leave this small town and go with her to a newly developed town to start a wonderful pastoral ministry there. She had a house under construction in Gangnam, the most expensive area in entire Seoul, and she used to hold a significant position in the megachurch, so I could not just ignore her proposal.

I asked her, "Why doesn't God tell me directly that he will use me greatly or order me to move to a new town?" "It is because you're not praying and spiritually dry these days," she replied and told me that she lives in a fancy apartment in a new town, but rarely sleeps at home because she prays all night in the church. It was not easy for a pastor, who prayed less than two hours a day, to ignore the deacon who prays all night. I was embarrassed to hear that I will become the greatest vessel in the Far East region when there were many excellent servants of God. Although I could not ignore her, I could not believe her words either, so it was hard to accept her offer.

I felt a sense of shame because I always heard about my next step from others. This was an unsolved mystery to me. I was not confident making up my mind, so I went to my parents and discussed the matter. They had already received a word from the Lord a few days before my arrival and said it would be much better to work with the deacon in the new town. They also shared a vision they saw while praying. I will not share everything here, but the vision was glorious that anyone would want to partake in it. Nevertheless, I could not leave the question: "Why am I the only one who always doesn't know God's will towards me?"

I did not hear directly from God, but I took it as a God's sign through his people around me, so I decided to start a new church. It was never easy to suddenly resign from the church I had pastored for ten years and plant a new one. Many gossips followed, but I took the courage to take action. My family moved into a 2562 square feet apartment with my parents. The apartment was in someone else's name, but it was agreed to use as a clergy house.

Among the church pioneer members, three other families were living in the same floor space as ours. Besides them, influential people joined us. We looked around some vast land to build our church and began to pray to establish a large mission center. Every week, we walked around the site of a college campus and a corporate training center next to the campus, which was more than 66,116 square feet, praying that we would be able to purchase the land.

If it worked out according to our plan, I believe we could have listed our church as one of the top five in the Far East. The newly started church was so visionary, and my passion was great too. However, although I was the leader of the church, I followed the vision given by others. I was sure that God called me a minister, but when it came to discerning the will of God, I always felt left out.

Get into a State of Confusion

Our church, which began with great aspirations, was in material trouble over the course of months. I did not consider thousands of dollars or tens of thousands of dollars as a lot of money, but we struggled because we could not get any less money than that. It was difficult for me and the church leaders to accept this situation. I thought there might be a problem with the members, but they seemed to think that this had happened because of my lack of power. We had to trust each other, but the situation drifted in the opposite way.

We started the church by temporarily acquiring a commercial building located in a nice area, which we could not manage. As things got bad and plans were delayed, I realized something had gone wrong. I was over 50 years old, and I did not expect the world to revolve around me, yet this was too much. It was clear that something powerful, whether God or Satan, was intervening in my life; one of them was my relationship with parents.

My parents and I quickly became estranged. It became so bad that it was hard to get worse than this. Then the unfortunate thing that should not happen occurred: my father kicked me out of this high-end apartment where we lived together in the cold winter. My family got a small farmhouse nearby and lived for about six months. Imagine living in a flat apartment with a wife and three children and moving to an almost collapsing farmhouse without any preparation; the house did not even have any heating system.

I went through so many ugly things that year; I felt as if all the bad luck for ten years came at once. My wife had no choice but to go out to work for a living, and my daughter, who was a college student, had to work part-time to continue her study. There was no spiritual or material help, and I felt like I was abandoned alone in this world. It seemed as if I had fallen into a trap that was impossible to escape, no I will restate that, I was already in it. Let alone my family, I had no idea how to live my life. The more I planned and implemented it, I was more sucked into a bottomless swamp. I was buried in grief thinking, 'Is my life going to end like this?'

PART 3

ENTER INTO THE SPIRITUAL WORLD

CHAPTER 14

SPIRITUAL PILGRIMAGE

Thinking of my family and church, I could not sit still. So I went up to the Cheonggye Mountain prayer house in Seoul, where I used to go often. One way or another, the pastor must find the answer in God. At there, my father did a long-term fast, and the head of the prayer house helped my father a lot when he built a prayer house. Our family has been close to the prayer center for decades. I was motivated to start praying again there. I shared a small room with another pastor.

One day I heard my roommate talking to his daughter on the phone. The pastor had a plan to build a new church building and wondered if it was God's will. The pastor's daughter said it is not God's will to build a new church building now; God said that when the next generation replaces the church leadership, he can construct a church. Wherever I went, people talked about "God's will."

When he hung up the phone, I had this and that conversation with the pastor out of curiosity. He was a pastor in Gwangju, Gyeonggi Province, and the church was growing by God's grace. The saints respected the pastor for his spiritual ability. He was ready to build a new temple, but he said he must seek God's will. After all, he could not build a new temple for the Lord just because he wanted to.

I asked the pastor if God really answers if we ask. The minister replied, "Sure, he answers." I have been dragged around by people, who claimed that it is God's will, but I had a hard time. I followed God's will, but I always faced problems and suffered damage, and even now, I was in that situation.

But now that I heard about God's will concerning other people's affairs, I could listen to it without any burden. I could trust his words because he had many fruits in his ministry. I asked the minister about the gift of the Holy Spirit since I brought up a question. Looking back, he did not have much spiritual knowledge, but he kindly explained by drawing a simple diagram.

He said there is a gift one level higher than the gifts mentioned in 1 Corinthians 12, which is the gift of communicating with God. He taught me that, one can receive the gift of communicating with God after receiving spiritual gifts, but it is also possible to receive the gift before receiving the gift of the Holy Spirit. In other words, saints can talk to God even if they can not heal diseases or drive out demons.

Since I read dozens of books on pneumatology, what he taught me was not new, but just by listening to his explanation made me want to pray again and desire the gift of the Holy Spirit; he was a good teacher.

Pastor Ahn's Guidance

After I came home, I visited a pastor Ahn and asked for help. Pastor Ahn had many spiritual gifts, so I used to call him "a man of supernatural." He always laughed whenever I called him by the nickname. I bared my heart to him and shared my thirst for the gift of the Holy Spirit, and my desire to meet God. He has ordained a pastor long after me, but since he was a senior in spirituality, I decided to follow his guidance.

My visit to him was a sort of confession that I wish to become a spiritual pastor again after twenty years since I spoke and sang hymns in tongues, encountered God, and attacked by Satan.

He teased me why someone like me, a Presbyterian pastor from a conservative seminary seek spiritual gifts, but he soon found out my sincerity and guided me spiritually. He said he had been everywhere for ten years to receive spiritual power. He knew almost all the speakers and evangelists on Christian newspapers and magazines to advertise their conferences. Also, the information about his spiritual world was surprisingly broad and profound.

He said, "Let's start all over again." We made a visit to various people of God with different gifts. When I acknowledged and accepted the spiritual ministry of those whom pastor Ahn introduced, he was delighted and laid the bridge to meet some more. We continued this spiritual journey for nearly six months. I can never forget Pastor Ahn for helping me and accompanying me this far.

During our journey, I sometimes received the Holy Spirit and fell backward, and I witnessed the wind of the Holy Spirit shaking people's bodies. At other times I received the prophecy and saw people receiving prophecies while holding a thanksgiving offering. One day, I went to a spiritual counseling center, which I had never been to, and what I experienced there was, in fact, amazing, but it was something that people in the conservative circle will freak about.

In particular, we received many prophecies from prophetic ministers. Because Pastor Ahn and I have always stood in line together, I used to receive the prophecy after Pastor Ahn. Surprisingly, however, the words of prophecies of famous ministers inside and outside of the county were consistent.

They prophesied that Pastor Ahn will minister for the youth and that God will give him a place to worship in the near future, and everyone said the same, no matter who prophesied, and it was done as it was told not too long after.

Whoever prophesied over me, the contents were the same. Ministers prophesied that God will pour his new grace and fresh gifts of the Holy Spirit upon me, and I would minister to those who are poor, weak, and sick. Some foreign ministers looked at me and said, "You are a very precious person." I was at a loss for the future and traveled around everywhere in spiritual hunger at the time, so whenever I heard such a statement, I was puzzled; frankly speaking, I did not believe it. Yet their words hit the mark.

I went to the Ganghwa Prayer House with Pastor Ahn during our spiritual pilgrimage. We wanted to receive prayer from the head of the prayer house, but there was a condition: we had to pray on the mountain for an hour. Both of us prayed out loud at the top of the hill. Sometimes, we prayed towards where the head stayed in order to win the favor.

The head told me that I am a good pastor and that God will give me grace if I overcome suffering. After my spiritual eyes were opened, I went there again. I met the deaconess, who was with the head on the first day I visited the prayer house. She shared what the head said about me: "By the time you almost arrived at the prayer house, the director said, a proud pastor is coming up, but he is a servant whom God loves." The head of the prayer house was a spiritual leader.

I attended an all-night rally held at the prayer house once a week. My overinflated ego was utterly broken at the meeting. If I were to say that I had made a pilgrimage to what the spiritual world was about up to that point, there I became wholly broken and humble. Whenever I went to a prayer meeting, I repented a lot. When the tears came out of control, I came outside and cried not to distract others. Then I wiped my tears off the tap, and went back to the rally; however, I burst into tears so often, I had to come out frequently. On the way home, I often made the atmosphere solemn because I could not stop crying in the van. It was embarrassing for a pastor over fifty years old to cry like this, but I could not help it.

Once when I was crying, a pastor whom I did not know handed me a note: "Be humble; when the time comes, God will exalt you." I knew he was praying a lot, so I trusted his words.

One day, while I was repenting, the faces of those who had conflicts with me when I was in pastoral ministry passed before my eyes; I was surprised to see their faces. I apologized to each person and asked them to forgive me. It continued for a quite long time. I saw the face of a fellow pastor and the faces of the elders and the deacons. Then, Sunday school students lined up and passed one by one.

As I repent, I realized how arrogant and sinful I was before God and to the people around me. I was ashamed of countless sins that I could not raise my head; I cried every day. The prayer house director, who saw me praying and crying all the time, said that the Holy Spirit's fire was burning inside me. He added that the fire burning inside is more precious than burning outside. Perhaps the outside fire referred to the burning of a person's body like a ball of fire, and the inner fire referred to sincere repentance. My body itself did not get too hot during the prayer.

I hardly went home for six months. After I came back from

spiritual or prayer meetings, I did nothing but repent in the church for several days. I rarely read books or newspapers; did not watch TV; did not use a cell phone; and I even pulled out all the church phone codes. I locked up the church door and prayed in tears every day. When my friends heard the latest news about me, they came to see me, but I did not open the door.

The mealtime came back pretty quickly, but I did not deserve to have meals. Does it make sense for a sinner like me to eat every meal? I did not eat full meals out of such remorse; I mostly cooked instant noodles and had them in the corner of the church office.

When I finished all the side dishes I had, I went to a nearby eatery and ordered lunch. There were almost always leftover rice or side dishes on other tables; whenever I saw them, I packed them home. I had never starved since young, but as one way of asceticism, I ate leftovers. I can not tell why, but tears rolled down my face as I had them. On the other hand, I was so grateful that I, a sinner, could eat precious food.

I kept praying and never stopped spiritual pilgrimage. In the course, I met many who always prayed and yearned for the grace of God. Our hearts became one and prayed together and held a rally taking turns. I adored the Lord with great enthusiasm. It was the first time that I gathered with pastors to pray and earnestly seek spiritual gifts, consequently, I had high expectations for this gathering, and it was so precious to me. I thought a lot about how nice it would have been to have such a meeting earlier.

The Holy Spirit manifested in a new way. When I met people, I naturally came up with what to say, so I wanted to pray for them; this prayer had a strong prophetic character. Also, I naturally spoke in tongues. I was very happy to have a new realm of spiritual experience.

I had many spiritual dreams too. Sometimes, I fought with a dragon that was big enough to not fit into my arms even if I hugged it with open arms. I prayed for more than ten hours a day on average and often prayed 15 hours a day. A long time ago, I heard about a pastor who prays for more than ten hours a day. At that time, I was so curious how such a busy pastor can spare time to pray like that. But surprisingly, I found myself praying for such a long time like him; I did nothing but look to the Lord.

Pastor Ahn introduced me to another new ministry. Pastor Kim in Incheon was famous for his ability to cast out demons. He lectured on Christian TV, and his ministry was broadcasted. Yet, it was unfamiliar to me when I heard that there are evil spirits in pastors since they are God's servants. But I trusted pastor Ahn and followed him, for I had wonderful experiences through him so far. When I laid down for the deliverance ministry, Reverend Kim pressed my eyes with his thumbs and said, "Fire," and my body began to get hot.

I have never had this kind of hot fire coming into my body before. I got so hot that I had to gasp for breath, and cried out, "Oh, it's hot!" I was amazed that such a strong fire of the Holy Spirit came through by his hands into my body. After a while, pastor Ahn pressed my armpit with his finger, saying, "Here is an evil spirit." Every time he pressed down on my body, I screamed in great pain.

Pastor Kim said there were not many people who he ministered in this way, "this is special treatment," he added. I tried to stand on my feet after 30 to 40 minutes of ministry, but I lost my balance. People told me it is because evil spirits left me.

Until then, I had never dreamed that pastors should also receive spiritual ministry; it was always saints who needed prayers and ministries. Moreover, I had a hard time believing there are evil spirits in my body. However, I stopped doubting because I experienced the ministry myself.

Pastor Kim gathered 20 to 30 people in one place and did a healing ministry. A sister who was obsessed with evil spirits kept talking in nonsense. I found this ministry very attractive because it drove out dark forces from people's bodies. My father was in the same ministry, but it came as a fresh blow for a pastor younger than me to heal people through deliverance ministry.

I thought of my family, relatives, and church members. I hoped that they too would be freed from evil spirits and recover. I introduced dozens of people to pastor Kim for deliverance.

I visited his ministry about ten times to observe the spiritual phenomena and stayed four to five hours each time; I gained a lot of new spiritual knowledge. I wanted to know the number of evil spirits that came in and out of people's bodies and how they looked like; however, I could not completely solve all my curiosities. Pastor Ahn led me to the prophetic ministry and helped me to experience the Holy Spirit, and pastor Kim opened my eyes to deliverance mystery.

Pastor Kim and His Wife

I started morning exercises for my health after early morning prayer with some members from the prayer meeting. One hot summer day, I had a chance to talk to a pastor, who was about ten years younger than me, while sitting on a bench resting. He resigned from the church a year ago under a false charge and was having time off.

I told him, "Don't be discouraged because you'll go through a lot in the ministry." I began to pray again because my ministry was in trouble, so I thought of my situation and said it in the sense of encouragement. When I shared about our prayer meeting, a gathering of pastors longing for the spiritual gifts, he listened with great interest.

His last name was also Kim, so I called him pastor Kim. I wanted to get him involved in our meeting, so I encouraged him to join us with many words. We went together to the prayer house I used to go to, and we visited spiritual people to receive prayers. He accepted and followed my advice well. And he sometimes attended our prayer meeting too.

One day, pastor Kim led me to a healing center in Chungcheong Province, saying he had somewhere to go with me. It turned out that he was a professor there. The contents of his lecture were mainly about "the way to the throne." His teaching was so profound that it surpassed all the spirituality and the spiritual gifts that I had been searching for; it was eye-opening, and I was startled. I felt ashamed of dragging such a great man around to receive grace. I wondered if I had made a mistake with him.

Pastor Kim knew I trusted him; he thanked me for treating him like anyone else because most other pastors looked at him with suspicion or considered him a spiritually dangerous person. As he said, nobody wanted to get close to him.

He also brought up about spiritual gifts. He informed me that I was spiritually ready but had no progression. He also said there are other spiritual gifts that are incomparable to the ones that appear to me now. At the end of our conversation, he suggested me to receive spiritual training from him. He had never made such a proposal to any other pastors around him, and I found his words true because I did not know anybody where he took me to train.

I accepted his offer because I acknowledged his spirituality. I told Pastor Ahn, who guided me so far, that I would not go anywhere for a while because I am receive training from pastor Kim. We had no reason to turn off the time, so a few days later, we began training at his home.

He first analyzed me through a vision, and his wife also prophesied to me with a vision she saw. There were two bridges as I am crossing the river; one was an old bridge at the bottom, and the other was a substantial new bridge at the top; she advised me to choose a new bridge. After all, the content of this prophecy was to go on the path of a new ministry that the Lord has prepared, which was the windup of similar prophecies that I received from other ministers.

Another minister from pastor Kim's center whose spiritual eyes are opened told me that I am a ministerial level in God's kingdom, and he said among those who he has diagnosed so far, my status was the highest. What I heard was exciting enough to clap my hands and dance, but it did not hit me at that time because I was still in trouble, and the gifts I had did not even measure up to the level of the ministers sitting in front of me. But at the same time, I heard similar prophecies many times before, so I could open my heart to his words.

CHAPTER 15

OPEN SPIRITUAL EYES

I began to repent intensively again at pastor Kim's house. Based on the Ten Commandments, I repented for serving other gods. Since it was all written in the Bible, I could repent without any doubt. Just because the Old Testament era is over, and we are in the New Testament era, it does not mean that all the sins of previous idolatry are automatically forgiven.

A few days later, pastor Kim and his wife laid their hands on me and prayed for me to open my spiritual eyes. About seven or eight people surrounded me to pray together. Pastor Kim again laid his hands on my head for one last time and wrapped up the prayer. It was an ordinary prayer that was not very different from the usual form of prayer, but God blessed me.

See the Heart of Man

When they finished praying for me, pastor Kim asked a deacon to stand up and made me close my eyes and see her heart. I could not understand what he meant, but I just closed my eyes and looked at the chest, thinking that a heart would be somewhere near there.

Soon I saw something that I did not expect: I saw a bowl of black water fluctuating, but it drained downward, and then the bowl was empty without any water. I shared what I saw in front of everybody. Pastor Kim praised me for what I had seen. Subsequently, he explained the meaning of the vision I saw. The water in her heart was black because she was confused and afraid, and the reason why water drained was that she was worn out. Anyway, it was surprising that there was a water bowl in the heart.

Evil Spirits

This time, pastor Kim instructed me to look at the brain. I closed my eyes and concentrated as he said. While I was thinking, 'Is it possible to see the brain inside the head?, the brain appeared in front of me, and I saw strange things wrapped around it. When I explained that I was seeing in real-time, he asked me to look more closely. I looked at her brain with my eyes closed, and I saw many threads of different shapes, some of which looked like a snake.

Pastor Kim was quite pleased; he asked me to ask the Lord the names of these threads, which were evil spirits. I have never asked the Lord anything, nor did I ever had any conversation with him. This was the most vulnerable part of my life, at the same time, a great wound. I was really ignorant about the spiritual world.

Asking a question to the Lord burdened me, "Will I be able to hear the Lord's voice or get an answer back if I ask him?" As I was thinking some evil spirits appeared in the form of flowers. There were big and small flowers at the tip of a slender branch. The moment I saw them, I knew that they were related to the shaman.

I had no idea what the flower had to do with the shaman, but I knew it was the spirit of the shaman for no apparent reason; my head and heart said they are the spirits of the shaman. Maybe it is because shamans like flowers and use a lot of artificial flowers that the Lord showed them in the form of flowers. Later I saw this shape in thousands of people. To test whether what I saw was correct or not, I commanded, "In the name of Jesus Christ, you, the spirit of the Shaman come out of this man," and the spirit moved and left the body. I have done these experiments thousands of times, so I can say for sure that evil spirits associated with shamans usually appear in flowers.

I also saw an evil force that looked like a "round ring." It was a simple expression of a scented bowl. Again, my head and mind said, 'This is the power associated with idols.' Pastor Kim asked me to draw evil spirits in other people's heads. I did not have any information such as names of evil spirits beforehand and had never sketched flowers, candles, or incense burners, but I just drew what I saw in front of my eyes. I depicted the evil spirits on the bodies of all the people in the place. It was not too difficult to draw visions in front of me than I thought. All those who were there were delighted to receive my sketches, and they were startled at the identity of the evil spirits in them.

Pastor Kim, who guided me, suddenly knelt and asked me to pray for him; I was so surprised and embarrassed; I have received prophecies from his wife and listened to his lectures. I respected them because they were world-class ministers. I have never seen a minister at this level before. I was thrilled and happy to have fellowship with them because they were close to God.

As I said earlier, pastor Kim was ten years younger than me, but I did not care about the age. I respected them and followed their guidance. When such a man knelt and asked me to pray, I refused, "I can't do that." However, he almost compelled me to pray for him, and it seemed like he would not back out, so I laid my hand on his head and prayed for him sincerely. I blessed him with all my heart. His body moved violently while I prayed for him, and he prayed passionately for more grace.

When I finished, his wife knelt and asked me to pray, so I prayed the same blessing. The other ministers who were present came up to me one by one to receive prayer. Everyone was very earnest and desperate when I prayed for them. I was puzzled by the unexpected situation; however, I prayed very powerfully because I was drenched in the Holy Spirit.

Later they told me that none of them were able to see evil forces in people's brains or bodies. They have never seen or heard of someone who can see and draw evil spirits so precisely like me. It has been a long time since then, but I have not yet seen anyone who can see evil spirits in detail like me.

I saw evil spirits through the gift of discernment, and I saw visions mostly through the gift of the word of wisdom and the word of knowledge. The gift of the Holy Spirit appeared strongly because I received their impartation after going through thorough repentance. Everyone was shocked by the gifts I received.

From the next day on, pastor Kim asked me to draw evil forces in people who came for healing and training. I met an average of ten people a day and drew what I saw in their bodies. I began to draw big and small evil spirits in various forms without hesitation.

Those who came to the center were happy to receive drawings of evil spirits in their bodies because accurately grasping the evil spirits affecting them was a great help when repenting. The people trained there envied me. I received an offer from pastor Kim to work as a paid minister at his healing center only after ten days I was trained there. As I joined Pastor Kim and his wife, who are already capable, we shined, and the number of spiritually desperate people visiting the center increased. I worked with them for two months.

See Sins of Others

One day, Pastor Kim laid someone down and asked me to see what sin he had committed. I closed my eyes and looked at the man, and a scene came to my mind. The vision was about his personal sin. I said it the way I saw it, and the pastor asked me to look at a few more, and the visions related to his sin continued. I needed a confirmation whether it was really his sin, or it was just my imagination.

I taught him what to repent, and he prayed on the spot. While he was praying, I kept watching the vision. Surprisingly, however, every time he repented, I saw changes in the content. For example, the man was a large log blocking the water, but when he repented, the log became small, and it disappeared later. I told him his sins are completely gone now. Every time I prayed for people, God immediately revealed their sins to help them repent.

Sometimes, I ministered to three people simultaneously; I saw a vision of each person and made them repent. I could see the progression of each person in visions; in other words, how well they were praying. When they finished praying, I told them another sin to repent, and I repeated this many times. I was so stunned at myself because I saw many visions in an instant; sent out evil spirits; knew immediately whether repentance had been made or not. Many people were surprised to see my ministry.

The Full Armor of God

Pastor Kim asked me to look at the full-body armor of the people who came to receive healing. Without fully understanding what he meant, I thought of a soldier in my head and gazed at the people with spiritual eyes. I saw people's shoes first. Some were barefoot, and others wore slippers, rubber shoes, sneakers, high heels, leather shoes, and military boots. Some shoes had their soles torn or shoelace untied.

I shared everything with people, and I believed that the Lord had shown me how well each person was equipped as a soldier of God. After seeing hundreds of people, I gained the confidence of what I saw when I compared my diagnosis and people's confessions.

An essential part of the armor was the helmet of salvation. People were wearing baseball caps, picnic hats, and simple helmets. Some were wearing perfect helmets used by the general, while others were wearing slotted or torn helmets.

Next, I saw the sword of the Holy Spirit, the word of God. Some had gigantic swords, and others had small swords. There was a person who had a tiny sword on a nail clipper. It seemed impossible to fight against evil spirits and win in spiritual battles with this weapon. In severe cases, some people had no swords at all. In other unusual circumstances, the swords were broken or fell to the ground; it seemed they became weak and attacked by evil spirits. There was a man with a huge sword but rusted, and there was a man who did not pull the sword out of the sheath no matter how evil spirits attacked him.

I also saw the shield of faith, the breastplate of righteousness, and the belt of truth in this way. The armors of God on people I saw with spiritual eyes were very precise. So far, I have diagnosed thousands of people and ministered to them based on it.

The Spirit of Murder

Once I ministered to someone who was very ill. When I looked at his neck spiritually, I saw a cable. I opened my eyes in amazement and looked, but there was no cable. I closed my eyes and looked at his neck again, and the rope was there. I scrutinized the rope and found that it was twisted with a speck of fluffy straw.

I pondered for a long time and realized that the cord around his neck was the spirit of murder, which appeared as a cable. The cable was twisted but looked like a new one. I wondered why the line looked new and found out that it represented the intensity of the spirit of murder.

I took a close look at the rope and found the line connected up and down. The cord connected to the top was wrapped around someone else's neck. The same was true of the bottom line. The three looked alike but had utterly different faces. At the moment, I realized what this was about.

The face at the top was the generation of this man's parents, and the one at the bottom was the generation of his children. The spirit of murder has been passed down in this family.

The condition of ropes that were linked to faces was all different: some were worn out and cut off, but some were strong and stiff. It implied that the spirit of murder working at his family had different effects on each family member.

I was a little shocked to learn that the spirit of murder was endeavored to kill people. Since then, I have looked carefully at other people to check if they were affected by the same spirit. In the worst case, some people had chains or metal ropes around their necks. Families with many short-lived and unnatural deaths had a strong spirit of murder like iron, and the families with the less or weak spirit of murder had thin thread-like lines.

When I discovered that the spirit of murder was influencing so many people, I wanted to know how it had entered each family, so

I prayed to the Lord, and he showed me visions for each person or family. For example, in a scene I saw, someone took off shoes and jumped into the water. I told my counselee that someone in the family had committed suicide, and that is why the spirit of murder entered the household. Quite a few times, I saw people hanging themselves. Suicide is also a type of murder that takes away one's life.

The spirit of murder also comes in by killing other people. Once, I saw a vision of a woman jumping out of the main room and fell to death in the yard. The woman was vomiting blood out of her mouth, and a man was standing in the inner room watching her dying. I had a hunch that she had been poisoned.

I explained why the spirit of murder was affecting each person through the visions that the Holy Spirit showed me. It helped many to repent their known and unknown sins, and made evil spirits to leave them much quicker. Sometimes, I was amazed at myself when I disclosed people's secret sins. But I had no other intention other than helping them to repent their sins and fight against evil forces. Only when evil spirits are cast out of our bodies and homes, the walls that were blocking us from God can break down and receive the full blessing of the Lord. Therefore, the saints must resist sin unto blood and fight Satan. I informed people of their sins precisely, and as a result, the center was filled with the sound of repentance and mourning.

The Sins in Building

One time, a pastor consulted with me because he wanted to pioneer a church. He was preparing a church in a 5,340 square feet building, and hoping to spiritually cleanse the place before initiating anything.

Although I never visited an actual site, I prayed to the Lord to ask what the pastor should repent relying on the floor plan. It was shocking to see so many evil spirits in each room.

I saw a scene of doing drugs in the room. Several people were getting shots in their arms and buttocks. I also saw a scene of sexual assault taking place in another room. In addition, in each space, scenes of countless past sins passed before my eyes.

I told the pastor everything I saw swiftly. He said he would repent and spiritually clean the place before he uses the building as a church. The people who previously lived there were unclean; I later found out who they were, but I will not reveal them in this book.

The Sins in the Land

Another pastor wanted to know if there were any great sins in the land before buying a building, so I asked the Lord. The building was located on a low mountain area, where it was presumed to have been used as farmland until recently. I looked at the vision without much pressure because I thought there would be no great sin on the land.

A man was walking down the street carrying a carrier on the back, and he was dressed in costumes from hundreds of years ago. Then there was an old man sitting on the carrier. The man carried the old man into the valley, and soon he left the old man, who seemed to be his father, alone and went away. It was a scene of an ancient burial practice whereby an elderly was left to die in an open tomb.

Whenever the Holy Spirit showed me a vision, it flowed like a movie rather than passing through each scene like a slide. Sometimes the film continued for five to ten minutes. Therefore, I could obtain the information on a particular incident from the beginning to the end. As soon as the pastor heard the land's sin, he repented of the sin on the spot. While the pastor was praying, I kept my eyes on the film before me.

Interestingly, the more he repented, the sin of the land lessened. When he repented sincerely, God forgave the sin of the land, and the spirits which entered through the sin left. Through this experience, I learned that even if someone has committed a crime in the past, it remains the same if nobody repents, and even if it is an old sin, it can be removed if someone repents. When the Lord forgives the sin, evil spirits can no longer stay.

Show a Demonstration

I visited the healing center, where Pastor Kim was a professor. He asked me to show people a demonstration of how to diagnose evil spirits after his lecture. There were about 30 to 40 trainees there, and I asked them to come forward one by one. Ten seconds was enough to see the evil forces in each person's brain. I drew the size and shape of the forces in the brain on the blackboard. One of them cried on the spot when he saw his spiritual state.

I asked everyone to repent for about ten minutes; then I drew their condition again to see if there were any changes. We did not pray for a long time, but when I looked again at the brains of people, it seemed that the evil spirits were weakened, and in the case of those who prayed sincerely, some of the evil spirits left completely. I became a spiritual star all of a sudden.

Offerings and Evil Forces

Among those who came to see me, there was someone who had committed a great sin. He had to invest a great deal of time to clean up his sins, and God required him of repentance offering. He decided to give offerings later since he was not in a good financial state.

He was not a member of our church, nor was he giving an offering to my church, so I did not care how firm he was determined to give. But as a minister, I was curious about the effect of repentance offering on the evil spirit. So I closed my eyes and asked the Lord what would happen spiritually when he gives an offering.

Then the Lord showed me one unique vision: an enormous dragon on the ground was tied to a rope and dragged into the sea. It could not move because it was stuck deep in the sea. I continued to watch the scene closely, and the dragon had his arms and legs tied with a string.

I learned the value of the repentance offering. In this case, it bound the dragon working against his household. If he does not give the offering he promised God, the dragon was likely to be rereleased from bondage. Thus, I advised him to keep his promise before the dragon is set free again. He was speechless to hear my words and said he would give to God as soon as possible.

A Building with Many Problems

A man came to see me for counseling concerning his building. He was building a communal house with other people. However, the construction was suspended due to the builders, who entered the building at their disposal and lived temporarily. He was in a situation where he had to pay a lot of expenses although he was not living in the building. He suffered from a significant material loss. He was desperate to figure out why this problem that is out of his control has happened. Since his building was built on expensive land, he said, he would like to sell the house and give it to God, if the problem is solved. Because of this building, he suffered from severe mental distress and prayed over it for many years.

I accompanied him to see the building with great curiosity. I prayed to the Lord to show me the spirits in the land and tell me why a person who is loyal to the Lord is under this hardship. I could see myself, in a vision, looking at the building, standing a bit away. An incredibly large fish appeared, which had an entire house in its mouth. The fish's teeth were so strong and sharp that it seemed impossible to escape. When I explained the vision, he was disappointed and afraid at the same time, because he intuited that the problems related to the building would not be resolved simply.

I tried to clarify the cause. The big fishes are usually related to the sea or river, and by no exception, the house was on the riverside. Fisher going out for fishing regularly held many rituals like "Pung Eoje", a ceremony for a big catch of fish on the hill, and this is what I exactly saw in the vision. The building was on the hill; it may look beautiful in our eyes, but it was actually a spiritually unclean place that played the role of "high place."

It is hard to be blessed by God because many evil spirits are already in place. Moreover, when people work or live in these spots, evil spirits either interfere or attack in various ways. I concluded that some repentance would not solve this long-standing sin. However, I told him that he and the co-owners of the building must repent thoroughly and cling to God, hoping that he would intervene. He asked me to pray for the property, but frankly, I could not.

Know the Condition of Fetus

One day, a man who could not understand his own behavior came to see me. He believed there was a problem with his character. I diagnosed him spiritually in many ways, and went a step further and checked what he was like as a fetus. Surprisingly, the Lord showed me what his state in the womb. I could clearly see and feel the feeling of a fetus. I saw how he was from one month to his birth and picked up things to repent and offered words of consolation if necessary.

Embryos have a profound influence on the formation of a person's character. Most psychologists claim that a person's intelligence and emotions are almost at stake before turning three, which I totally agree with. The problem is that evil spirits often attack the fetus: it gets attacked when the mother sins and when it responds to it in sinful ways. During infancy, evil spirits gradually settle down in the body, and they exercise a decisively negative effect on character formation. This is something we all go through as we grow up, and no one is an exception. Therefore, all believers need to take time to pray, looking back on how they were spiritually in their prenatal years, if possible.

It is Possible to See Unconsciousness

God knows every single thing concerning us. He knew us when we were in our mother's womb and even before that. Thus, God is conscious of lives on this land as well. He knows what we say and how we behave. Furthermore, he is well aware of our innermost thoughts, and even our unconsciousness that we do not normally perceive.

As I mentioned in one of my books, *Heal My Lamb,* we can see what is hidden in other people's hearts once our spiritual eyes are opened. For example, assume that you have hidden someone you love or hate in your heart. Even if you have never told anyone about it, a spiritual person may know the secret in your heart. In my case, I can see who people like or dislike, and help them confront their issues if necessary. The responses of those who received this ministry are almost the same: they are flabbergasted, and say, "The Holy Spirit indeed searches all the deep thing of our hearts.

There should be no one but God in our hearts. Jesus Christ is the only master of our hearts; he must only reside in the inmost place of our heart; no one other than Jesus should be allowed to stay there.

Spiritual Black Hole

When I first started the deliverance ministry, I thought a lot about where to send evil spirits. I can see whether they are still left in the body, or on the way out, or if they are entirely out. It is crucial to cast out evil spirits from the human body, but it is also essential to clean up the spirits that came out of the body.

In the early days of my ministry, I sent demons to the mountains, sea, and sometimes to the shrine. If we do not drive them away completely, they either stay in the air or enter another person. Therefore, it is essential to cast out evil spirits not only from our bodies but also from our surroundings. There is the best place to send them: to the cross of Jesus Christ.

"Sending evil forces to the cross" means sending them to the Lord. Then the Lord locks them up. The spirits that have been driven out to the Lord can no longer stay on the earth, in consequence, the number of evil spirits existing on the planet decreases.

Every time I send demons to the cross, I see them going up to the sky and flying 5km to 10km. But one day, they disappeared right beside me without any trace. So the next time I drove them out, I carefully watched where they are going, and saw a black hole next to me. I saw evil spirits sucked into the hole, and could never see them again. However, it varied from time to time. Sometimes, evil spirits went far away, and at other times, they disappeared right next to me.

I had no idea what was happening, so I ministered dozens of times, hundreds of times in the same way. Some evil spirits went straight into the black hole, but some others kept sticking their heads out to escape. In this case, I commanded them to get in the hole again. I later found out that fully repented sins usually disappear right away, but ones that lacked repentance had the strength to keep themselves out in the air.

Through this, I experienced that the kingdom of God is not far away and that this world in which we live is part of God's kingdom. The Holy Spirit is in us and near us. Just as evil spirits can travel from this world to the spiritual world in a moment, the Lord can also come to us in the blink of an eye. It does not take hours or days for the Lord to come to us from his heavenly throne when we pray.

Bitter Roots in the Body

There is something that must be done before driving out evil spirits: it is repentance. The sin of serving idols, in particular, must be more intensely and thoroughly repented. Exodus 20:5 tells us never to worship idols: "You shall not bow down to them or serve them, for I the LORD your God am a jealous God, visiting the iniquity of the fathers on the children to the third and the fourth generation of those who hate me." The sin of idolatry affects the offspring as well. It is an illusion to think that the transgression will disappear by themselves after three or four generations.

If the descendants continue to serve idols without repenting the idolatry of their ancestors, the sin will snowball and affect the next generation. That is why the first generation of faith usually suffers more than those who have believed in God for many generations. This is the spiritual principle: families or people who are in God are blessed, and families or people who serve superstitions and idols are cursed. This contrast becomes more apparent over time.

I once ministered a woman who was considerably clean because she went through deep repentance. But one day, while I was ministering, I saw her heart wide open, and there was a tomb in it. Then the grave was opened, and a coffin appeared. I was frightened at the sight, but when I came back to my senses, I examined the coffin carefully. I did not realize on the spot, but I later figured out that this coffin was representing "the spirit of death."

The vision continued, and many people came out of the coffin in a row. I was so surprised that I opened my eyes and then closed them again. I could still see people coming out of her heart in a long procession with flags as if they were holding a funeral.

These forces in human form were evil spirits that had entered her body as a result of her ancestor's idolatry for many generations. The evil forces carried flags to reveal when they entered. I watched the funeral procession for a couple of minutes. When she eagerly repented for her ancestor's worship of idols, the funeral procession moved quickly, and when she prayed slowly, they moved slowly. I was very confuddled since I had never heard of any story that is similar to what I was witnessing, but the Holy Spirit helped me to grasp what was happening.

It took about an hour to finish the funeral procession. When the ministry was over, the lady said she felt a huge void in her heart and felt light. I told her it is because many evil spirits were driven out.

With an inspiration of the Holy Spirit, I named this ministry "the bitter root": our bodies are made of soil, and just as the trees are deeply rooted in the ground, evil forces are deeply rooted in our bodies. It is especially true for the evil spirits that have passed down from generation to generation; they are black, strong, and active.

Thankfully, my wife, daughter, and several other ministers who were there witnessed the same sight. We were all amazed and saddened at the same time, for we witnessed how dreadful sin is.

Generational Spirit

There was a man, and he wanted to pray for the sins of his family. His brothers were married, but each of them was undergoing many hardships. As the eldest son, he wanted to repent his parents' sins and bring peace to his brother's families. He gave me a repentance offering and asked me to pray for him. Since he loved his family and prayed much of his sins, I gladly decided to pray for his family. I offered an offering to God and prayed that God would take his wrath from them and that they would be at peace.

As I prayed, I saw evil spirits working above his family. It is difficult to put it correctly, but it looked as if there were dark clouds. I looked into the clouds and saw evil spirits, big and small, tangled with each other.

They were staying above the family because of the sins that were committed until now, and they were holding back the blessing of God. These evil spirits were also preventing the prayers from ascending to God. They were affecting people belonging to this family in the air.

If saints repent with a genuine heart over these generational spirits consistently, the forces will divide and gradually move away, and through the gap, the grace of God will come down, and the prayers will also go up to heaven. Although all the dark clouds that cover the air cannot be removed or dealt with utterly, making some gaps between heaven and earth through repentance itself is a great achievement. We must break down the walls that are blocking us from God.

At someone's request, I came to see this generational spirits. I also saw groups of evil spirits above other families; their forms and natures differed depending on the content and quantity of their sins.

There were spirits above my family as well, and I repented over them whenever I had time. Shamefully, many generational spirits in my family were related to grumbling, anger, and blocking the path. Because of these spirits, my parents and siblings were attacked a lot, and many problems that we could not solve occurred. Above all, they incited us to commit similar types of sins continuously.

Angels Work

If one can see demons or evil spirits, he or she is likely to see angels too. Satan was originally an angel, but he fell and became an evil spirit. During the deliverance ministry, I saw angels taking away evil forces; angels bigger than the size of evil spirits came and took them. When repentance was riped, angels easily bound evil spirits because they had no strength, but when repentance lacked, angels had to put more effort to take them. In the case of powerful evil spirits, angels bound them with ropes in order to take them.

I also saw a lot of healing angels. There are not only big angels but also small angels. I saw a small healing angel touching the sore part of a saint. When spiritual eyes are opened, we can see angels in action everywhere and can get familiar with the spiritual world. Since the spiritual world is so vast, there are always things to uncover.

CHAPTER 16

SPIRITUAL HERITAGE

I helped pastor Kim's ministry for two months, and I came back to my pastoral site. I had no choice but to break up with pastor Kim because I started my own healing ministry in addition to pastoral ministry. Since they decided to go abroad, I had a brief conversation with the couple before they left.

Pastor Kim admitted that God granted me unusual gifts. As I shared the journey of how I received these gifts, I came to talk about my parents. He said that the reason I was able to receive precious gifts from God is 80% because of my parents, 10% because of my efforts, and 10% because of his guidance. In that sense, he asked me not to forget him; I promised to do so. Pastor Kim finally said, "There is a man of God who is more capable than you," and advised me to be careful not to lose spirituality, since I can subject to become arrogant by performing many miracles in the future.

Because I ministered with the couple for the past two months and received grace from them, I took his advice seriously. Although he did not introduce me to a person who he said is more capable than I, he mentioned pastor Doo-Sup Um, a writer of a book called

Scent of Spiritual Life. In this way, we went in a different way. A few years later, I heard the heartbreaking news that pastor Kim had passed away at a young age.

My Father's Gifts

As mentioned earlier, my father has served as a healing minister for over 30 years. He mainly healed demon-possessed people and prayed for those who were ill, such as cancer. I grew up watching his ministry bearing many fruits. After my spiritual eyes were opened, I diagnosed his gifts in curiosity; the gift of healing and the gift of working of miracles appeared strongly.

My father particularly had a substantial gift of driving out demons. In the past, I could not understand why demons became quiet before my father. Evil spirits cannot go insane in front of those who have given the power to cast them out. God also gave me this power, and demon-possessed people become gentle when they are brought to me. There is no way to explain this except that I have inherited my father's gifts.

There is one thing I discovered while talking to my father after I got to know the spiritual world. He had the experience of healing a person with spasm from being demonized. He said whenever he ministered the person, strangely enough, he felt something like a spider web always covering his head and body. When my father shared this with several pastors who visited the prayer center, they casually said, "Maybe it's because there are many cobwebs here and there."

However, since there was no spider web found anywhere in the prayer center, my father was puzzled. Nobody came up with a clear answer or an apparent explanation. Ten years later, when he saw me taking away the cobweb-like spirits from a man's body, he found the

SPIRITUAL HERITAGE

answer himself. He said that what I experienced was not entirely new and that he had already experienced it a long time ago. At that time, I was struggling to analyze what this was about, but my father had already figured it out; there's nothing new under the sun. Given the length of time mankind has existed on the earth, there will not be an entirely new thing.

Because my father had the gift of discernment, he could feel the small spirits attaching to his body, although he could not see the precise shape of the evil spirit, for his spiritual eyes were not deeply opened. It can be concluded that my father was strong not only in expelling evil spirits but also in discerning spirits. By God's grace, I can see and even touch the evil spirits in addition to my father's gifts. I always thank God for his unutterable grace, for he granted me priceless heavenly gifts upon the tremendous spiritual heritage I have received from my parents.

I was able to devote myself to prayer because my father was a good model of prayer. As mentioned in previous chapters, he prayed a lot on the mountains, and always went to church at 11 p.m., and led the early morning prayer meeting; he continued this life for decades. At that time, I could not understand him, and I often spoke in a critical tone who would volunteer to do the ministry if one had to do it like my father. But now I pray for at least three hours a day on average, and more than four to five hours a day while ministering countless people. When there is no ministry, I often pray for about ten hours.

When people come to see me on a day when I pray quietly, I honestly am not happy with them. Even if I have to meet people, I always try to simplify the business and quickly return to the place of prayer because it is precious and pleasant to be around God. On the contrary, when I face people, I am influenced by the evil spirits in them. Therefore I believe that it is always more beneficial to seek God than to hang out with people for no particular reason. Some might ask back how one can socialize if one does not get along with people, but their opinion is not important to me.

My father had been the head of the prayer house for nearly 20 years, but he had never invited a speaker to hold a rally. He did his best to guide each person who came up to the prayer mountain, and I am also ministering in a way that heals and teaches individuals. My father's precious gifts and his ways of ministry affected me a lot in many ways.

To sum up, because my father and I are in a close relationship both spiritually and ministerially, if anyone criticizes my father's experience, it is nothing short of criticizing me. And if anyone doubts my ability to discern spirituality, it is like questioning my father's thirty years of ministry. I had walked a completely different path from my father until my spiritual eyes were opened, but now I am walking on the same path with him as a "spiritual minister."

My Mother's Gifts

My mother was a seer and had a gift of prophecy. When we first started a prayer house, she foresaw the view of the prayer house in a vision. Surprisingly, we started a prayer house in the same place that my mother had seen. Since God showed visions when she prayed for the saints, she prayed prophetically over them. I believe that God gave her this kind of grace because my mother was a woman of prayer. She fasted and prayed for 40 days, even after she was 50 years old. At times, she prayed for several days or 15 days without drinking any water, and then fasted for another 20 days drinking water if it got too tough. But she never spoke proudly of this. In addition to these special prayers, she kept her prayer life thoroughly.

I sometimes got phone calls from my mother; she told me in advance about the difficulties or good things that are to come. Whenever I talked to her, I felt grateful, but on the one hand, I felt like being watched. I had no choice but to be conscious of my mother, who prayed in fear and trembling before God, and I, too, had no choice but to try to pray earnestly.

My mother tended to be more neutral than feminine; she was very tough, bold, and adamant. She always raised me so strongly that she never held my hand and hugged me. My mother repeatedly said, "No matter what difficulties you may face, don't look at men, but look to God." I was given the gift of seeing visions, the gift of prophecy, the gift of strength and boldness, and the gift of not giving up through my mother.

Her way of education became a constitution for me, and there was a great advantage. I raised three children in the same way, and I take the same posture when I train and guide God's people.

Spiritual Gifts from the Parents

Among the many spiritual gifts, the gift of discernment, the gift of deliverance, and the gift of doing miracles stand out in particular. Besides, I see visions, prophesy, and draw evil spirits delicately. Based on the nine gifts in 1 Corinthians 12, numerous other gifts appear to me.

Thousands of people who seek spirituality have visited my center so far, and countless times have been told that no one has ever seen evil spirits as well as me.

Especially, I see evil spirits in the body in great detail. Thousands of people had come to my healing center so far, and I was told countless times that they have never seen somebody who sees the spiritual world at my level. Assuming that I pray in tongues for 100 people; the tone, the color, and the accent will differ each time I pray. I am also amazed that I can speak in tounges so diversely.

However, I am well aware that I did not receive these outstanding gifts because I am worthy; God granted me more gifts that he had given to my parents. Even after I became a pastor, I had no interest in these gifts for a long time; I did pastoral ministry like everyone else. Looking back, I lived a lot of years in spiritual loss.

Although I opened my eyes to the spiritual world and participated in healing ministry in my fifties, my parents were proud of me at the fact that I succeeded and finally acknowledged their ministry. But in essence, they probably have liked it because they valued this ministry. Therefore, my parents prayed for me every day to receive more gifts of the Holy Spirit.

No one is as blessed as I am because I have gifted and spiritual parents who pray for me. I believe that my parents' prayers and spiritual energy have flowed into me, which strengthened and deepened my spiritual gifts. I am grateful that these gifts will flow down to my children. I genuinely wish my children to live as God's servants like me. My parents lacked in some ways, but I thank them for living spiritual lives.

CHAPTER 17

START A HEALING MINISTRY

My Face Brightened

I lived in a fantasy, like walking on the cloud after my spiritual eyes were opened. Every day I said, "Thank you, God." For I lived in the presence of God, I lacked nothing.

To be honest, most Korean pastors wish to pastor in a large church and be respected; I was no exception. I lost interest in the world, and my desire to have a successful ministry was gone. I was grateful that God has given me gifts so that I could live as a man of God. My face brightened because my heart was full of joy. My church members told me in unison, "Your face brightened." People from outside the church said the same thing.

I started to pray again because of various problems at home and church, especially financial problems. They were not solved immediately, but the way I view them has changed. Meeting the Lord and seeing the spiritual world thrilled me as much as I have gained everything in the world.

But I could not tell everybody that I can see the spiritual world. Even if I told my acquaintance what I had experienced, they all replied, "How is that possible?" In this atmosphere, I could not go on with a more in-depth account.

The fellow workers who prayed together for the fullness of the Holy Spirit responded the same way. Frankly speaking, I was very disappointed with them because I expected they would react differently from others since they are spiritual people. They prayed and asked for the heavenly gift, but they did not even know what they were asking. When the amazing power of God manifested, they were surprised and retreated.

Yet, one thing I was grateful for was that most of the prayer house leaders and spiritual leaders whom I had met to learn more about the spiritual world acknowledged my gifts to some extent. Some of them asked me to impart them with the same gifts God gave me or came to me for training. Those only who knew the spiritual world valued me.

Pray for People at Dawn Prayer

The members of our church longed for the gift of the Holy Spirit from the beginning, and since they knew that I also desired for the gift, they were very excited and acknowledged what Holy Spirit doing in me.

As many great gifts manifested through me, they began to respect me more. Most of the saints who attended our church used to hold important positions in other mega-churches. Even before I received the power, they recognized and trusted me, but somehow they seemed to think that I lacked something. So in the meantime, when I gave any advice or guidance, they sometimes did not seem to take it with humility or obedience. But when I became potent, their attitudes changed dramatically.

One day, after the early morning prayer service, a saint came up to me and asked for prayer. He had to make a very important contract today. It was the first time that a member of my church asked me to pray. He laid a cushion and knelt in front of me; I prayed with my right hand on his head. I did not often lay my hand on the saints, but this time, I was confident that God will work through my blessing.

When I prayed for him, I saw a vision concerning him as if I see a movie. I asked him if he wants to know what the Holy Spirit showed me; he wanted me to tell and explain everything openly. In a vision, a black train was heading into the cave; entering the cave symbolizes hardship. However, the train derailed and rolled to its side even before entering the cave. God's servants must speak just as the Holy Spirit reveals. His complexion turned bad. Although he intuitively understood the message, and he asked me back, "What do you mean?" I told him what he expected.

When I finished praying for him, another saint asked me to pray. Every time I prayed for people, I had visions. It was the first time in 20 years that I saw visions when praying for the saints. If fellow pastors question me if it is necessary to see a vision while praying, I will reply that it is "better" because it benefits the saints more, in a sense that pastors can be well aware of the spiritual condition of their congregation and give them more practical advice.

I saw visions regardless of my will. From then on, I had visions whenever I prayed for people. Visions usually contained the spiritual condition of the person receiving the prayer, the things to repent, and the changes after repentance. The number of saints requesting for prayer has increased gradually.

Every dawn, I prayed for each and every saint. They brought their family members or relatives to the church to receive prayer or for spiritual diagnosis. They were proud of me and proud that they were the members of my church; they praised me wherever they went. The ministry got busy; in addition to general duties, such as preachings, visiting houses, counselings, I added the spiritual ministry. As a result, I was able to serve people more diversely.

House Cleaning

People invited me to their homes, churches, and workplaces for spiritual cleansing because they knew I could discern the evil spirits in the building and sins of the land.

Some houses had evil spirits in the living room, in the main room, and even in the veranda. Usually, the spirit of poverty appeared in its original form, which is a snake, but it also appeared as an empty can or fleshless fishbone through the gift of the words of knowledge; the spirit of murder appeared primarily as a sword or a rope; the spirit of luxury appeared in colorful clothes, and in the case of the spirit of violence, I saw people fighting to each other. God revealed evil spirits in each house, and I shared what I saw with people, in order to give them the list of sins to repent. Since evil spirits have entered the house legally, there is no other way but to repent to expel them permanently from the house.

While cleaning the church, in a vision, I saw a small ditch on the church site and people catching and killing dogs. Perhaps people have killed dogs in this place since long ago. I came out of the church and looked at the terrain, and was more convinced that this place was used for that purpose. This can also hinder cleanliness.

I once visited a church in a basement with the ministry team. Several evil spirits were sticking their heads out from the wall toward the church. So we spent some time analyzing and repenting sins in the space with the pastor. Then when we commanded them to go out in the name of Jesus, they began to retreat.

It is spiritually beneficial for the church for evil spirits to leave the church. We must know that the reason why evil spirits are in the church is to ruin and fail the church. When evil spirits are cast out, their presence disappears, so people entering the church may literally feel lighter and fresher. Also, since the main forces which disturbed the saints are gone now, congregations can concentrate on prayer, and receive the word of God in a more accepting atmosphere. If evil spirits do not hinder the church, the saints can grow faster.

Those who think that evil spirits can not stay in the church because it is a sanctuary are beginners who are not familiar with the spiritual world. There is no place without God, and there is no place without Satan's power either. In the past, evil spirits established idols in the temple during the Old Testament period and made Judas Iscariot, a disciple of Jesus, to hand over the Lord to soldiers. We must remember that Satan approached Jesus, the son of God, and even tested him.

Satan is not something that we should be afraid of, but it is a dark force that we should not ignore. These evil forces take place where there is sin and exert their power; it can be human bodies, houses, or churches; there is no exception.

Sense Evil Spirits Stick to My Body

I studied for seven years in seminary, lived as a pastor for twenty years, yet I did not know much about Satan and the forces of darkness until I was over fifty. It was only after I opened my spiritual eyes that I realized Satan and his followers were not the imaginary enemies but the real entities among us all the time. Evil spirits basically have transparent shapes like small threads. The small ones are like slender threads, but the larger ones are in the form of snakes or dragons that are in the Bible.

I have so far preached countless times about Satan, demons, and evil spirits, yet I never knew that they are so close to us, and even reside in our bodies. For those who are not spiritually sensitive, dirty, or spiritually blinded, can not sense the evil spirits in the body and outside the body. Therefore, it is difficult to live conscious of their existence.

There was one thing that bothered me so much when I became clean through repentance and spiritually sensitive as my spiritual eyes are opened: I felt evil spirits covering me when I meet people. I felt quite uncomfortable, and sometimes it was even painful. The reason they could approach me was that I also had a similar kind of sin.

Above all, living in the same house with my family was the hardest part. My whole body ached after I came back home from visiting my parents. Families are most likely to be exposed to the attack of evil spirits, since they share the same nature of sin, and are close to each other. So I sit at a distance when I talk to my family. People may criticize my attitude, but I have no choice but to keep some distance until every family member becomes clean to a certain extent.

I sense evil spirits now, but they were there all the time. Since they transfer easily, I had many evil spirits that are from my parents in my body. If my parents had repented a lot, they would not have harmed me this much spiritually, but unfortunately, that was not the case. Although they prayed a lot and had the power of God, they did not repent regularly. I told my parents the sins they should repent and encouraged them to repent not only for the sake of themselves but also for the whole family.

If I meet people who live according to God's word and have

not sinned much or those who repent on a daily basis, I am rarely attacked by their evil spirits. Even if they stick to me a little bit, I do not suffer much because their strength is weak. However, meeting unrepented people is painful for me. I feel very uncomfortable and distressed when I travel by public transportation because evil spirits in people are so strong.

As a result, many changes occurred in my life. I did not meet people for as long as I could. I met people who came to me for counseling or healing, but besides that, I avoided unnecessary contact and spent a lot of time with the Lord. Perhaps, monks might have avoided meeting people for the same reason.

Start Ministry

The first target of my spiritual ministry was my church members. Many of them had attended a large church or mega-church previously, but they were spiritually thirsty. That is one of the main reasons why they came to my church, but over time, they were disappointed a little bit because they were not satisfied here either. Therefore, when I was filled with the Holy Spirit and received the gift of the Holy Spirit, they all rejoiced with me. They brought other family members and relatives to me for ministry.

I have served the church for 30 years, including years that I served the church as an evangelist, but this was the first time I was recognized and enthusiastically welcomed by the saints. People regarded me as a servant of God. People came to see me, so I did not have to be busy going here and there to meet people. I felt like this was how the minister of God should look like, and how pastors should serve God's people.

I did not have major shortcomings: I was born in a Christian family; graduated from a good seminary in Korea; preached well;

had excellent interpersonal relationships. In addition, I held many vital positions in the presbytery. I had a lot of experience in the church and studied in Seoul from elementary school to graduate school.

But when I became acquainted with the spiritual world, and God's power manifested through me, the things that had previously been strengths were no longer highlighted. To be honest, when I compare myself to what I used to be, the things that used to stand out looked very ordinary. The reason why people came to see me and respected me was evident: I have become a "spiritual leader." The grace God has given me somehow became a significant factor that distinguishes me from others in general pastoral ministry.

I watched my father drive out demons and treat the sick since young, but because I had never tried on my own, I had no idea and had a lot of trial and error, when I first stepped into this ministry.

Minister My Families and Siblings

Another first target of my new ministry was my family. I helped them to repent their sins and drove out evil spirits in them. Although it was a very sudden and unexpected suggestion, I thank my sisters and brothers for trusting me and accepting my ministry.

I also trained them; within a few months, their spiritual eyes were also opened. Because they had spiritual heritage from the parents, many gifts appeared as they made themselves clean. All I did was help their unactivated spiritual gifts to rise to the surface and guide them to take an interest in the spiritual world. After all, my effort was minimal.

Then I met a couple of pastor couples who have been friends for more than decades. I shared with them how I have come to see the spiritual world, which was a result of living a reclusive life focusing on prayer, especially repentance, for almost a year. Most of my friends did not believe me, and even those who somewhat believed in my testimony were not willing to repent or showed interest in my ministry; only one friend wanted to have his spiritual state diagnosed to repent.

I also delivered the news about me to those who have prayed with me for the past six months. Some of them gave me full support, bringing their whole family and dozens of saints to me. However, most of my prayer comrades were wary or dubious of my account, probably thinking that I went too far. No matter how fervently I explained there is a way to open spiritual eyes, they seemed unwilling to listen to me. We became estranged since we could not get on so well.

Over the course of time, many people came to see me. More than a hundred people, 20 people each from five of my sibling's church, came to the healing center. In addition, some of my friends brought people, and some who heard about the ministry came to the center for healing or spiritual training. As a result, the healing center was packed with people. I consulted more than 10 people a day, and 32 people visited me at the most.

I mainly did one-on-one ministry because I watched the whole process of evil spirits going out; it helped me to concentrate and accurately diagnose the problem. I believe knowing every detail of what is happening spiritually is the proper way to minister. Imagine how hard I have lived ministering each person for an hour.

 I went to work at nine in the morning and came home after midnight. As far as I can remember, I did not take a single day off from the healing ministry. Because I was grateful that the Lord has given me grace, and people continued to come, I was willing to work restlessly. On the one hand, I was sorry to the Lord because I was spiritually ignorant for the past ten years and wasted my time on less important things.

People came to me for a variety of reasons, and I chose a ministry that was suitable for each person. For example, some were ill with an unspecified affliction. Doctors could not make a prescription because they could not figure out the cause. In this case, it is usually the spiritual one. I did not send a single person without any feedback. I told them what conditions they were in, and what sins they should repent, and after taking some time to pray, they came back for deliverance ministry. Most of the time, people were healed and went back to their daily lives. I have often seen people rolling around and having seizures as demons left them.

Those who were physically handicapped by evil spirits were also healed. People wanted to know how they were spiritually and physically, so I gave them accurate information through various diagnoses.

Many involved in the spiritual ministry and other ordinary people wanted to know what kind of gifts they have, so I wrote down about 40 to 60 gifts for each person. There are many evil spirits in the human body, but there are also many gifts, both general and spiritual, from God. Some others wanted to know how the Lord considered them, so I received and delivered the word of the Lord. Also, people wanted to know the sins of their ancestors. Nothing was impossible for me when it came to spiritual matters.

Various people visited me, including high-ranking officials, chaebol families, those who passed the state examination, teachers, and oriental medicine doctors. Besides them, pastors who served large churches, pastors in foreign countries, and missionaries who have worked hard at the mission field for decades came to see me.

It was only a year ago that I was challenged and went up the mountain to pray, but now I have become the top-notch minister whom many respects. All this was like a dream to me, however, since it was God's absolute grace, I always try to stay loyal with a humble heart. There is nothing to boast about me.

Those who have worked as professional healing ministers for ten or twenty years came to me for spiritual diagnosis. They repented and received or deliverance ministry. They envied my gifts of discernment and the power to drive out demons, but at the same time, they realized that God gives amazing gifts to people who live in this age.

Countless believers have come to me with a strong desire to see the spiritual world, and I helped them as much as possible. In a year, about a hundred people were fully trained at the center for two or three months.

Change the Target of the Ministry

By counseling and ministering to numerous people, I felt that it is essential for people attending church to undergo spiritual diagnosis and repentance. Only then can the saints escape from the stronghold of evil spirits. However, realistically, I can not serve all Korean saints by myself. This is not only impossible in time and strength, but many people in different denominations will refuse to trust me. Even if one of the mega-churches in Korea acknowledges me, I can not cover them alone.

It was heartbreaking to think that many people of God in Korea will never have an opportunity to go through genuine repentance, and never know how evil spirits attack them while living in this world. If I continue to serve laypeople, my church may revive, but my gifts will not benefit the entire Korean church.

About six months after starting the healing ministry, I asked the Lord to raise a hundred more servants of God like me because I concluded that more believers will get chances to repent and get close to the Lord if more ministers at my level are established. Since then, I have set the pastor's family, the minister, the missionary, and the evangelist as the main target of my ministry.

The Lord was pleased with my request and promised that he would allow the gifts he has given me, not only to a hundred but to even more people. I get excited just by imagining this promise coming to fulfillment. Honestly, it is very lonely to do this kind of ministry in the mainstream of Korean churches. Therefore, meeting leaders and an increase in the number of ministers in the same ministry with the same heart is always encouraging. Jesus had all the power and ability, but he never worked alone; he built God's kingdom with his disciples.

I led people who came with a passionate heart by all means. So far, God has used me as a tool to build nearly 600 people instead of 100. I can not confidently say that all of them received the same level of gifts and abilities as mine, but God has officially set up over 70 healing centers across Korea to date of writing this book. There are unofficially 30 to 40 more centers, which makes 100 centers; they are all doing the same miraculous ministry. Since each center not only heal people but also imparts and trains the gifts of the Holy Spirit, the impact and synergy are enormous.

My wife's family has been a family of faith since Christianity first came to Korea. She is helping me a lot with the ministry now, but she hesitated at first because she could not discern whether it was right or not, and it created many frictions in our relationship. But by the grace of God, she also decided to repent and fell face-down before the Lord. As a result, God opened her spiritual eyes. It is a bit off the point, but statistically, clean and straightforward people tend to gain clearer spiritual sight. My wife has become the most reliable companion, and we are working hard together for the kingdom of God.

When I worked alone, I had to put a great deal of time into the ministry, but with the help of my wife, I could take some time off. We have also become able to work more effectively, complementing each other's shortcomings. I grew up watching God's work sometimes hindered by the conflicts created by my parents because both were capable ministers. Therefore, I did my best not to make the same mistake, so we could bear more fruit.

Although I had a few church members and did not earn a lot of money, the amazing work that God has accomplished through me has been so great that it can not be compared with revival and material. I have the word of John the Baptist, which I have kept in mind for years: "He must increase, but I must decrease"(John 3:30). I always tried to bear the burden of any loss or sacrifice if it pleased the Lord.

CHAPTER 18

ESTABLISH SILOAM MISSION

From January 1, 2005, I have put my mind to a new ministry for a year and greeted the New Year; more than ten people were healed and opened their spiritual eyes, and more people acknowledged my ministry as biblical and they valued me. I was in agony since I lost a lot of friends and materials, but I was able to make new spiritual friends.

I longed for this ministry to spread at home and abroad. As one means to this end, I needed a meeting where ministers could get together to socialize, pray, and do spiritual ministry together. After discussing with people around, I decided to set up a mission. The hallmark of our ministry lies in "holiness through sincere repentance." Everyone has sins that they remember. Yet, more crimes are committed unconsciously or unknowingly, and most of them are unremembered. Therefore, for individuals to be thoroughly cleansed, they needed to know their sins through the ministers who have the gift of the word of knowledge and the gift of discernment. The church must teach both believers and unbelievers the need for repentance, along with the gospel of Christ.

When the saints become holy through repentance, God gives great power. I personally hope that all the saints become holy enough to fight Satan and build up others. Today, many saints often groan from spiritual or physical illness. So I named my ministry "Siloam World Mission," modeled after Jesus' healing at the pool of Siloam.

Also, in 1985, which is 20 years ago, the first church I pioneered in Jangan-dong, Seoul was also Siloam. At that time, it did not mean much because the name was given by another pastor, but when I think about it now, God meant me to do the Shiloam ministry. And in 1990, which is 15 years ago, I wanted to organize a mission, but it was canceled because I planted a new church unexpectedly. I found two treasures which I had lost for years at once: the name Siloam and the Mission.

By the grace of God, Siloam Mission and its ministry grew year by year. Many spiritual people and healing ministers were trained, and the movement to restore the Korean church and the saint through repentance spread out. Thankfully, more than 570 people have been formally trained until recently. I joined the Korean Association of Independent Churches and Missions in order to launch a more full-fledged spiritual movement. Siloam Mission has more than 100 public centers, both officially and unofficially. I believe that the Lord will extend this ministry further in the future.

CHAPTER 19

PARTING AND SEPARATION

Alienated from Old Friends

My family members and siblings supported my ministry, and most of them also saw the spiritual world through my ministry and training. I am grateful that my family is walking on the same path. I give glory to God for the grace he has given us and for using us as his vessels.

While some families, who share the same faith in Christ, have many scholars and others have many pastors, I would like to say my family has produced many healing ministers.

I feel pride in this because one can not open their spiritual eyes with great wealth; it is only possible through the grace of God and thorough repentance. Seeing the spiritual world and receiving the gift of discernment have historically been allowed only to a few people.

Unlike my family, who welcomed me, about half of my prayer partners, friends, and pastors refused to acknowledge my gifts; everyone was reluctant to accept me or not. They were uncomfortable with me mostly because my spiritual eyes were opened, which means I could know the secrets of their hearts and the sins which they wanted to keep to themselves. Some were eager to meet me, while others did not want to see me at all.

I once diagnosed the spiritual condition of pastors who attended a regular prayer meeting together. Most of them heard the news that my spiritual eyes are opened, but it seemed that they were having a hard time believing it.

I knew they had a great passion for spiritual gifts and powers, so I truly hoped that they would also receive the gift of the Holy Spirit. However, few people approached me to figure out how I got to see the spiritual world.

I could see how spiritually everyone was, in what state and situation they were in, even with my eyes open.

One day, a family invited me to visit their house. The lady of the house offered me a cup of tea; at the moment, I unconsciously saw a knife in her womb. The size of the sword showed me the size of the spirit of murder. The blade in the uterus was a hint that any kind of life-threatening surgery was done in the past. I was not careful at the moment and said, "I see a knife in your belly." "Don't look," she said in astonishment and embarrassment.

I was a novice in spiritual ministry at the time and could not bear to say what I saw. A professional minister must deliver the contents of any kind of ministry when only individuals want to know, but I made a big mistake because I brought it up without any consent. After I made this awful mistake, the rumor about me spread, and even those who recognized me did not welcome me as before. I admitted my mistake and tried to be careful ever since.

Meanwhile, I raised another problem. There was a missionary who withdrew from the mission field after working hard for God for many years and started a new ministry in Korea. When we were having a conversation, he said, he had lost consciousness while exercising and fell backward. I paid attention to him since then because I cared for him. I invited him to my church to hold a prayer meeting. He kept walking around on the pulpit while preaching, and it looked odd in my eyes. When I asked him about it, he insignificantly replied that it is just one of his preaching habits.

However, I thought his action was worth studying spiritually; I was curious if his behavior had any relation to his spiritual state. When we gathered to pray together after the sermon, I saw his brain momentarily. The forces that entered when serving other gods occupied 70 percent of his brain. I always ask this question when I see people with this much evil spirits in the brain: "Do you have a shaman in your family?" When I told him with a loving heart that there are many evil forces in relation to shamanism in his head, his complexion changed, and our prayer meeting has become very awkward since then. The way I delivered the content was very wrong, but the content itself was critical.

I had a lot of friends from college and seminary. They were exemplary pastors who bore many fruits in their ministries. We had been friends with each other for more than 30 years. However, as I became spiritually sensitive, I felt uncomfortable in socializing with them.

When I had fellowship with my friends, some of the evil spirits in their bodies were attached to me. Also, my mind was full of thoughts about "repentance," so my heart was troubled when they talked about worldly things. And there was no reason for me to spend time with people who disapproved of me. Spiritual people should spend a lot of time with God; when we hang out with people, we often end up wasting our time.

From my friends' point of view, the fact that I was the only one who could know their sins could not have been pleasant when there should be no faults between friends, and we could not continue a serious conversation because we could not find much in common with each other as we used to. Also, since I was the only one who could see the spiritual world, my friends might have felt a sense of difference. For one reason or another, we become estranged from each other. Sometimes I thought about them, but it was not easy to contact.

My previous church members came to see me from time to time. But they felt distant from me because I was not as comfortable as I used to be, so they stopped coming to me and calling me over time.

My hometown is Seoul. My friends from elementary school who lived in a neighborhood were scattered all over Seoul, but they did not contact me because they heard the news about me. Some friends visited my church, but I have become estranged from most of my friends. A friend once called and said: "Pastor Han, are you ascending and descending the heaven these days?" with a mixture of envy, jealousy, and doubt; I just laughed off.

In the meantime, some people recognized and encouraged me, so I was able to overcome the loneliness. What is more thankful is that I have countless new friends now who are spiritually awake. We are living in a spiritual age, and I am sure that the new fellow workers and I are standing together at the core.

Leaving Presbytery

After receiving the gifts of the Holy Spirit, I devoted myself to the healing ministry. It was very rewarding and fun to work with my wife, to put it differently, this ministry was perfect for our constitution. I often thought about how much more I could have pleased the Lord not wasting any time and how much more my pastoral ministry would have shined if I had my spiritual eyes opened when I was younger. But as we all know, everything does not go our way. I am grateful that I can be used by the Lord even now.

Some people in my presbytery challenged my ministry, which I have fully foreseen. I was in a conservative denomination, so it was natural for them to have a negative attitude towards my ministry. I was well aware of this atmosphere because I belonged in the circle for more than 20 years. I did not expand or advertise my ministry since I did not want to be suspected or criticized by them; however, it was destined to be known one day.

Few of the presbytery members congratulated me on receiving a great grace from God, but because some people raised questions against me, people debated over my ministry. All pastors will feel burdensome when their ministry gets on the chopping block at the presbytery. People debated whether the gifts I received were from God or not; some argued that I was possessed by evil spirits; some others said my mind is sound but my ministry is suspicious. I became the subject of suspicion, and it was hard to bear.

It was an issue that could disgrace my parents, my siblings, and my children. If pastors misjudge me, my whole family could be stigmatized. It was all the more critical controversy since my family and siblings were involved in the same ministry.

The presbytery tried to look at my problems fairly. First, they set up a committee to interview me and thoroughly listened to my opinion. They also offered me a chance to talk to my alma mater professor. I also sent letters to some professors, explaining my ministry, and received answers. I thank my fellow workers for taking these reasonable steps for me. My case would have been concluded without a proper process of the investigation if it had been another organization.

It is all in the past now, but it left much to be desired in that nobody made a visit to my healing center upon my request for more accurate judgment.

The content of my interview was known to the presbytery members, and when the presbytery was held, they discussed the matter again. I could hear everyone's statement because I was there too. Some claimed that it was God's grace, and some others said they could not believe me. I decided to respect and accept the outcome no matter how it turns out because they had given enough thoughts for my ministry.

I came home in the middle of the meeting because people wanted me to leave. The presbytery members debated until late night and threw a vote on whether my ministry was appropriate or not. And I was admonished not to do this ministry anymore. I heard later that the decision was made 15 to 13, and many had abstained. In order to follow the presbytery's guidance, I had to give up my ministry since they regarded it inappropriate. But the fact that nearly half of the people supported my ministry even though I was not there was a great comfort. To assume that I am in a position to evaluate someone else's ministry when a considerable number of people are raising issues and the person directly involved is not present, to be honest, what good would I have by defending or acknowledging the person? In any case, every decision comes with responsibility.

After the decision was made, I met some pastors who were there that night. They all suggested me to leave the presbytery and do ministry freely. Some of the senior pastors I admired had the same opinion. And a professor, a spiritual ministry expert whom I respected, encouraged and supported me not to give up this ministry, saying that the healing and spiritual ministry is essential in this era.

I have always followed the presbytery's guidance until then. However, the gifts God gave me was so apparent that I could not stop the ministry to follow their counsel. I do not claim to be one of the religious reformers in church history, but throughout church history, I learned that the man of God respects freedom of faith and conscience. Therefore, as much as others have the right to judge me, I believe that I also have the right to choose my faith in God unless it is not biblical.

However, if I stayed and continued the ministry as a member of the presbytery, it was evident that they would put pressure on me again. I did not want to create conflict further. If only I give up my membership, there would be no problem. So I formally sent my withdrawal to the secretary before the next meeting. It was right for me to give a finish to the work officially, for they had many debates over me. And I included in the document that I would wait without joining another denomination until the presbytery recognizes my ministry. The presbytery accepted my withdrawal, and I was removed from the list.

Four years have passed since then, and I have kept my word so far. But now that I have started a church in another area, there is no point in keeping the promise. In the end, I lost my close friends, denomination, and presbytery by doing the ministry God wanted. But I still keep in touch with many of them personally. When we walk with God and devote ourselves to the entrusted mission, we should not expect to be welcomed and embraced by every people around us. Yet, all ministers must walk by faith with confidence because God gave each of us different tasks on this earth.

PART 4

ADD DEPTH TO SPIRITUALITY

CHAPTER 20

SPIRITUAL EXPLORATION

Begin to Read Books

When I was in the graduate school of theology, I was very interested in systematic theology. So, I participated in a systematic theological society. I read Louis Berkhof's books in class and read all of Hyung-Ryong Park's books on systematic theology as an assignment. I was particularly interested in "pneumatology." My father was a healing minister since I was young, so as I grew up seeing him healing people, I became interested in the Holy Spirit.

If everyone had the gifts of the Holy Spirit, healed sickness, and cast out demons, I might not have been attracted to study on the subject. However, my parents longed for spiritual things since I was a child and received the gift to heal people. Yet, I was confused because some professors at the seminary refuse to recognize the gifts of the Holy Spirit. Among those who recognized the gifts, none of them clearly taught me about the gift my parents received. Between theology and reality; parents and professors; I needed a judgment of third-party.

For this reason, I spent a lot of time buying and reading

ADD DEPTH TO SPIRITUALITY

numerous books on the Holy Spirit during my seminary years, trying to come up with my own conclusion. As I studied on the subject, I discovered that the positions regarding the gifts were divided into two groups. One side insisted that the spiritual gifts still manifest powerfully today, but the other side claimed that they do not appear anymore, and some even viewed people who minister with the gifts as heretics. But neither side held a dominant position, and the argument was in a tight line.

As I was attending a conservative seminary while my parents were partaking in healing and deliverance ministry, I found my attitude quite lukewarm. If I raise my parents' hand, I would have a different opinion from most of my friends in the seminary, and if I choose my school and friends, it meant my parents were abnormal; thus, my position was really ambiguous.

While reading numerous books, I was comforted by the writings that claimed the Holy Spirit is still working, and the gifts still appear in this era. It assured me that my parents' ministry was biblical and that the spiritual experiences I had were also biblical; I could easily find evidence as much as I wanted in the church history.

At that time, I was doing a general pastoral ministry and did not receive great gifts yet. On the inside, I believed in the gifts of the Holy Spirit and his wonderful works, but I continued to preach, pray, and visit church members just like other pastors. Although I had a few spiritual experiences, I could not jump right on to the power ministry.

But at the moment I am writing this book, I have already received wonderful gifts, and my calling has become evident; nothing is standing in the way now. I am no longer conscious of those who doubt the gifts and suspect people who manifest the gifts because they are not God, and they are not the subject who gave me a vocation. How can I stand with people who oppose the gifts and works of the Holy Spirit when the powerful gifts are manifesting through me? From my point of view, to make the spiritual knowledge known to the world and to show the power of God to the world is to live according to my calling.

I devoted myself to reading for quite a while. After the ministry, I regularly read books on spirituality and the Holy Spirit. Since I had little time to go to the bookstore, I bought 30 to 40 books when I had a chance.

From the day I opened my spiritual eyes to the present-day, I have read about 350 books. Even if I wanted to buy more books, I no longer felt the need to buy books because the contents of the books were all similar. I still go to the bookstore with expectations, but I often come back empty-handed. If there are books dealing with a new and deep level of spirituality, I would love to buy and read them. I mainly read two kinds of books: one was about the spirituality of monks, and the other was about the ministry of apostles and masters of healing.

My dream was to accept and grasp all spiritual phenomena that have appeared in Christian history. I wanted to be a person who knew everything and could answer with assurance, no matter who I talk to or what spiritual subject I talk to the other person.

Everyone has their own goals and desire to be the best in that field, and I am no exception. I have a desire to be known in the world for spirituality and the gifts of the Hoy Spirit. Not because I am after fame, but because I want to be honored and used before God in mighty ways. I am always running towards my goal, even at the expense of many things, to achieve my dream; dreams should not remain unfulfilled. I would like to introduce some books that readers can easily find among the books I have received a lot of help reading.

Books on Spirituality

In Korea, there are not many world-famous ministers like western countries, so I had little expectations, but I was impressed a lot after reading the writings of Reverend Hyun-Bong Kim and Jung-Pyo Lee. Reverend Yoon-sun Park's commentary has been of great help to me as well. I took his class and was greatly influenced by his sermon. But the person who shocked me the most after my spiritual eyes were opened was Reverend Doo-Sup Um. His book *Scent of Spiritual Life* challenged me. The book mainly said that Korean Christianity is currently too weak spiritually and that Korean churches will have no future just as European churches if we do not go through some reformation. While reading his book, I was grateful that there is someone like him in Korea who strengthens the root of Christianity, pursues spirituality, and teaches spirituality in-depth.

I read Reverend Doo-Sup Um's *Yeongmak: Core of Spirituality,* and was shocked again. Although I have repented sincerely, I realized how much deeper I had to look back on myself and deny my old self before Jesus Christ. I was ashamed that the saints, including myself, were busy seeking after worldly things rather than seeking heaven, and tried to build our own castles high in this world.

Through his writing, *The Barefoot Saint,* I learned about Hyun-Pil Lee, who returned to God's bosom after living a pure and modest life. Every time I think of him, I feel small; I tried to eat less because he only had a minimal amount of food; I also ate food that fell on the floor to humble myself. At every kimchi-making season, I had new members at my center go to the local field to pick up some cabbages and radishes—then we cooked with the discarded ingredients and had meals all winter. *Saint Francis, To Come After Death,* and *Wind of the Holy Spirit,* by Reverend Um have also fundamentally transformed my perspective.

As I continued reading writings on spirituality, I learned how the monks lived after reading a book on St. Anthony. I could understand why he was exalted as a saint. His life, such as living in the desert, fighting with demons, practicing isolation, teaching people, and treating the sick from time to time, has rekindled the fire in my heart and desire to live like him.

Also, the spirituality and power of St. Benedict impressed me; the monastery rules he wrote for monks were beneficial. I was moved by Avila's Teresa and Jeanne Guyon, who remained steadfast in the face of persecution. In addition, I read the biography of those who had influenced each era at random, and my heart burned with fire. I discovered that because God loves the church and the world, by his grace, he sent spiritual people to reform the corrupted churches in each age.

I was interested in Henry Nouwen's spirituality, so I read several of his books. Although he was a precious man equipped with everything, he always humbled himself. From his life, I learned that the people of God today should live like him. I liked Thomas Merton's books as well.

What I found after reading many of these books is that Protestantism is less interested in spirituality than Catholicism. After Luther's religious reforms, Protestants abandoned monasteries. However, the spiritual movement is inseparable from the monasteries. Even if Protestants want to initiate a spiritual movement, there are not many leaders who can present vision and lead us.

Realistically, Protestant pastors are systemically forced to spend a lot of time on sermons, running church programs, and church politics; thus, it is not easy for them to pursue deep spirituality.

I have constantly been reading books about spirituality for a while. I enjoyed reading E.M. Bounce and Richard Foster's writings. Of course, Jonathan Edward and John Owen are indispensable. I also read Leonard Sweet's *Out of the Question - Into the Mystery* interestingly. J.C. Lyle's *Holiness: Its Nature, Hindrances, Difficulties, and Roots* is a must-read book, and C.S. Lewis' book is already well acknowledged.

I also read Catholic books: I read *Catholic Traditions and Christian Spirituality* and *Spiritual Theology* by Jordan Orman, which was very helpful, containing profound spirituality. Also, *The Coming of the Cosmic Christ* by Matthew Fox, *Spirituality and Justice* by Donal Dorr, *Living in Abundance - The History and Theology of Christian Spirituality* by Josef Weismayer, and *Ascent of Mount Carmel* and *Dark Night of the Soul* by Saint John of the Cross, *Interior Castle* and *The Way of Perfection* by Teresa of Jesus, *The Breath of Mystic* by George A. Maloney, *The Wind of Nothing Blows in Prayer* by Shigeto Oshida, *Contemplation and Personal Revelation* by Hyo-Ik Bang, Meister Eckhart's books on spirituality and Sister Lucia's memoir *Fatima*.

Among the books covering spirituality and mystery, Dionysius' *The Mystical Theology* and *Pseudo-Dionysius* provided an opportunity for me to think deeply about things I had never pondered before; they contributed significantly to my spiritual experiences and theories.

While I was at it, I also read the stories of Syrian priests and Celtic spirituality. I had no idea that Christianity has pursued such a variety of spiritualities. I believed that I would become a good pastor by reading and studying the word of God, preaching the word, and taking care of church members; I thought I would become a great person if I receive great gifts; I believed that I would succeed if the church revives in number. But the most fundamental thing in the ministry was whether I have an intimate relationship with God and walk with him every day or not.

Books on the Gift

Spirituality and the gift differ in meaning: I want to define spirituality as the way of living life before God, while the gift is a powerful and special present from God.

Gifts are divided into general and special gifts. The gifts that appear in 1 Corinthians 12 are the root of special gifts. Yet, spirituality and gifts are inseparable and cannot be strictly distinguished. They will be discussed in more detail in Chapter 21.

I wanted to know the fundamentals or principles of the spiritual world while doing healing ministry. In other words, I wanted to learn more about God, angels, and Satan. Dr. Ho-Sik Kim's *The Angel of God* and *The Fallen Angel* helped me a lot. I am sincerely grateful to him for revealing spiritual beings systematically.

And as I read Charles Kraft's *Deep Wounds, Deep Healing*, I fundamentally understood the relationship between spiritual war and healing. This book has become a textbook for my ministry. And by reading *Defeating Dark Angels*, *Rules of Engagement*, and *I Give You Authority*, I have laid the framework for spiritual warfare and healing ministry. Without these books, I would have spent more time to have certainty in the spiritual world.

I began to read the books of Peter Wagner, who is close to Charles Kraft. I have acquired vast knowledge regarding evil spirits and applied them in actual ministry from his books *Prayer Shield*, *Prayer & Spiritual Warfare*, and *Breaking Strongholds in Your City*.

I read Neil T. Anderson's writings with an interest in evil spirits. His writing has been translated into several volumes in Korean. My alma mater professor Hwa-Ja Yoo of the Hapdong Theological Seminary was interested in this part and translated *The Bondage Breaker*. *Breaking Through to Spiritual Maturity* is also a great book. I believe his writings have been of great benefit to the Korean church.

Professor Yoo might have been suspected and criticized by some of the conservative denominations in Korea because of his book, *The Spiritual War and Healing,* but he has become a pioneer in research related to the spiritual war for he took the risk.

In several books, I discovered that evil spirits enter the bodies of the saints, causing diseases, furthermore, intellectual disabilities, and emotional problems, which led me to have more confidence in my healing ministry.

There are many people who present theories about the ministry of healing and are actually involved in the ministry of healing. The book that helped me to comprehend the principles of the healing ministry is Peter Horrobin's *Healing Through Deliverance*. I recommend this book as a must-read for all healing ministers. There are quite a few people in Korea who have studied this field, including *The Holy Spirit, Healing, Ministry,* by Pastor Myung-Geun Oh, *Clinical Pastoral Studies,* by Pastor In-Hwan Han, and *Principle of Praying Against Adversary* by Pastor Won Jeong. They have made considerable achievements in the barren land.

I bought all ten books of the "Power" series from Nathan Publishing and read them all in a flesh. This series teaches well how the church of this era should move forward; in short, the church must restore its ability.

I began to buy and read books about the evil spirits in the

household because I found evil spirits operating in each house. I read Yun-Ho Lee's *Win the Warfare of the Generational Blessings and Curses,* Marilyn Hickey's *Break the generation curse,* and Derek Prince's *Blessing or Curse, You Can Choose.* These books are criticized within a conservative theological framework, and I do not accept everything either, but I can not deny that I received some help from these books.

For people suffering from deep inner wounds, I read *Now I Know Why,* published by the Christian Family Affairs Center. Among Duranno's Christian counseling series, I also recommend books on depression, self-esteem, and self-control.

I wanted to go a step further and study the world-class figures who fought against demons and devoted themselves to heal people. Antony the Great and Benedict of Nursia, the founders of the monastic movement, are one of them. They were genuine seekers of God who exercised their powers while seeing the spiritual world, and they were the ones who stirred up the spiritual movement of those days.

I studied church history again from the beginning. I have seen many spiritual figures organize spiritual movements in each period to purify the church and strengthen the faith of believers. Among them, many healed the disease. In the 20th century, Smith Wigglesworth and Kenneth Hagin were representative figures. Kenneth Haggin's *I Believe in Visions* served as a driving force when I went through repentance and sought after spiritual gifts. This book made me have a passion for the spiritual world. I bought about a hundred books of Haggin and distributed them to the people around me. If you want to know more about masters of the healing ministry, Roberts Liardon's *God's Generals* is the best one.

There are also formidable objections to spiritual ministry

around us, but if you read William L. Arteaga's *Quenching the Spirit* and *Understanding the Devil* from Eounsung Publisher, you will see how futile their claims are. A few years ago, I read Nam-Soo Kim's book, *God's Love and Healing Ministry,* which I recommend because I received a lot of help regarding the principles of spiritual and power ministry.

Through reading, I realized that the church in the future, like the early churches, must demonstrate God's power in the word and healing. Wagner's friend Ed Silvoso's *That None Should Perish* also made my heart passionate.

Watch the Videos of Healing Ministry

In the early days of my ministry, I did not know how to do the healing ministry; the most typical type was the one my father did. In the meantime, I visited several other healing centers and experienced the healing ministry myself, yet it seemed my father's ministry was the most effective one. I wondered if there were any healing ministry or spiritual ministry at a higher level, so I researched and explored here and there. I wanted to study how the ministers of God around the world heal in different ways.

One day, someone gave me a bunch of videotapes. Among them, there were videos of Cathryn Kuhlman. I was able to see and learn about her healing power and the extent of her ministry through the videos; I also watched several videos of Benny Hinn.

Their ministries were different in many ways from my ministry. Although their methods could be seen as a part of the healing ministry, they were not a new model. I can not judge or evaluate them; however, I believe that they would also agree that their ways are not the best ones.

I have searched for people seeking spirituality or doing healing ministry in Korea. Some of them had considerable power. I personally had no chance to meet them, but it was certain that the Lord was using them.

Spiritual Music

During my spiritual pilgrimage, there were songs I enjoyed singing at the church and prayer center besides hymns. In the church where I pastored, we have only sung hymns. Therefore, I was not used to singing gospel songs, and sometimes it even felt burdensome. However, as I repeatedly sang gospel songs, I felt my heart opened and softened.

My prejudice that only hymns are the true praise has gradually disappeared. After my heart was softened, I realized that I was only rational and lacked sensitivity, let alone spirituality.

Now, whenever I sing and listen to the praise songs, whether a hymn or a gospel, my heart gets warm, and joy overflows. There is a song that I personally sang over thousands of times. When I was spiritually blind, when I repented, and when I finally opened my spiritual eyes, I always sang the same song in tears. The song is called *What the Lord Has Done in Me* by Reuben Morgan:

> Let the Weak Say I am Strong
> Let the Poor Say I am Rich
> Let the Blind Say I Can See
> It's What the Lord Has Done in Me.

This praise always touches me because I feel like the subject of the song. I was weak, but now I am spiritually strong; I was poor, but now I am rich spiritually and materially; I was spiritually blind, but now I see the spiritual world. By the abundant grace of God, I am what I am now.

    Since then, I have enjoyed singing hymns. I found spiritual songs among contemporary Christian music or gospel, and always played them during prayer hours. I had a lot of time to pray, listening to praise songs because I rarely went outside unless it was a special occasion; naturally, I came across many spiritual praise teams; one of them is *The Tent of David,* led by Scott Brenner. His team praises as if they are at the throne of God.

CHAPTER 21

SPIRITUALITY AND SPIRITUAL GIFTS

As mentioned earlier, Korean churches tend to have weak spirituality. Although the book introduced spiritual ministers in Korea, they fall behind compared to world-class ministers. Unfortunately, no person in Korea can be advocated as a globally influential prophet or minister.

The Korean church has gained worldwide fame in terms of church growth; almost all the big churches of each denomination are in Korea. There are many reasons why Korea has been able to form such a big church, but I think one of them is the leadership of the pastor. However, an increase in the number of church members does not necessarily mean that the church or the church leader is spiritual. It is because pursuing spirituality and carrying out spiritual gifts based ministry is a little different area from growing the church.

There are many great preachers and pastors in Korea who have revived the church. However, there have been few pastors and saints who share deep friendships with God. In addition, there are many large and small healing centers in Korea, but few have been exposed worldwide. There are many reasons why Korea falls short of spirituality and healing, but I think the biggest one is that Korean church pastors and saints are extremely busy.

We must become one with Christ, as Calvin said. Just as the bride and groom share their own secrets in the bride's room, the faithful saints must share a deep friendship with the Lord.

However, Korea's pastoral environment is poor in this respect. First of all, the problem is that so many churches are competing against each other for more members. Since most churches operate independently, they often have financial difficulties, and a considerable number of pastors live on incomes that fall short of the minimum cost of living. In this environment, it is challenging for a pastor, who has to take economic responsibility as a head of household, to put everything down and look only at God. Nor do the saints allow the minister to stay before God putting many church ministries behind.

In fact, large churches or small churches are all too busy, without much difference. Busyness and spirituality are poles apart. To pursue spirituality, one's relationship with God must be the top priority, and all other things must be secondary. It is almost impossible to have a deep spirituality while being busy in the world and busy with the church programs. The monks who lived in the wilderness seem to be lazy and unproductive if seen with the worldly perspective, but they do many things to attain more spirituality.

The second reason for the lack of spirituality in Korean churches is the lack of repentance. There is a widespread belief in Korean churches that all sins are forgiven, only if we believe in Jesus Christ. It is a strange concept that if one believes in Jesus and repent once that one does not need to repent again. This is a doctrine advocated by the Salvation Sect, which is one of the significant heresy in

Korea, but strangely, the Korean church has partly accepted its core doctrine unknowingly.

No one is unaware that Great Britain's Welsh Revival in 1960 or the 1907 Great Revival of Pyongyang began with repentance. Yet, if we encourage to repent the sins of our ancestors and our own sins, strangely, not many believers are willing. Many books on the work of the Holy Spirit says that the first step in receiving the Holy Spirit is repentance, but when I ask people to repent, many of them are stubborn to repent. I do not understand when some people treat me as a weirdo only because I said, "We have to repent." Unfortunately, we may be a generation that lost repentance.

Since it has been less than 150 years since Christianity was introduced to Korea, the history of Christianity in Korea is very short. In the case of most Korean families, almost all the families served the foreign gods in their great-grandparents or great-great-grandparents. Therefore, it is not easy to produce a world-class minister in this spiritual environment, where evil spirits are powerfully operating based on idolatry.

I observed closely at the foreign ministers who relatively have fewer prayer hours than Korean pastors. They received many gifts and great powers, even though they did not strictly observe the Sabbath or attend prayer meetings. As a result of my research on this matter, they had a lot of spiritual heritage since they had faith in Jesus for a relatively long period of time and had fewer sins of serving foreign gods. As a result, there were fewer walls or evil spirits, blocking them from God compared to the Korean ministers. Ministers from the Western world usually have a spiritually good environment, which allows them to draw close to God, although they do not put a great amount of time in prayer.

On the other hand, it is difficult for Korean pastors and saints to have an intimate relationship with God without great effort because of their sins and generational spirits even if they want to be close to God.

Therefore, while Korean pastors can revive the church and deliver brilliant sermons, it is not easy for them to become a top minister in the world. At this point, Korean churches should also have something spiritual to offer to churches in the world. We have been famous for the revival and the mega-church, but I think it is time for the Korean church to become famous for its spiritually outstanding figures. Korea has many top-notch industries around the world. I hope Korea will stand out as well in spirituality as any other field.

The Gift Can Appear Even When Spirituality Is Weak

Gifts and spirituality are originally one, but everyone usually sees them separately these days. It can be said that spirituality is the one that moves closer to God, while the gift is the one that moves toward man. In Korean Protestantism, spirituality appears more often in the direction of gifts, which includes nine gifts of the Holy Spirit. Most ways to receive the gift are to pray fervently or be imparted by someone who already has the gift. If there is any distinction between the gift and spirituality, it would be that one can receive the gift of the Holy Spirit to some extent if one asks for it, although he or she is lack of holiness and purity to draw near to God.

Korean ministers and revivalists prayed a lot to receive spiritual gifts, and it worked quite well. In other words, they were able to receive power despite their weak spirituality. We all witnessed the falling of great ministers due to ethical and moral issues. We all try to understand them by thinking, 'they are human too,' but I say that more real causes can be attributed to their weak spirituality compared to the gifts they received.

The Deeper Spirituality Is, The More Likely to Receive a Strong Gift

It is obvious that the people who received spiritual gifts have put in a lot of effort to gain them. If believers lay down themselves and focus on purification rather than merely asking God for the gifts, this too can be a great way to receive power. Saints who simply ask for power may encounter limitations, but if the purpose of prayer is to purify themselves and become holy as God commanded, not only the spirituality of the saints will deepen, but in most of the cases, the gifts of the Holy Spirit will naturally follow. In this way, saints can have their cake and eat it.

However, most Protestant ministers do not seek deep spirituality and tend to prefer the power and gifts over spirituality since they are more visible to others. All believers must first be sanctified through repentance to have a high level of spirituality or the ability to overcome temptation. Only then can the evil spirits be weakened, and we can be less affected by them. If we draw close to God, we can possess the incredible power of Jesus Christ because we are his bride. And, like Jesus, we will be able to serve God's kingdom powerfully.

CHAPTER 22

GO THROUGH REPENTANCE AGAIN

I was annoyed by the tickling of evil spirits on my body after I became spiritually sensitive. In particular, I felt threadlike evil spirits moving on my head 24 hours a day and 365 days a year. It has been seven years since I lived in this condition.

Pierce Through

As I repent, the forces inside penetrated my body in order to go out. Once big forces are all gone, only small ones come out, but they sometimes reach tens of meters. Although they are small, if repentance lacks, it will not be cut off. In such a case, a string-like force can be pulled out by hand and then cut off.

I have done all sorts of things to remove the evil spirits from my body as much as possible. Sometimes I put evil spirits on a pole and went around and removed them, and sometimes I attached evil spirits on a passing car to go far. However, after a while, they got disconnected on the way, so I had to pull them out with my hands again. Believers can just command evil spirits to leave, but if one has power, one can touch and pull out evil spirits as well. I have done this for years.

If anybody sees me pulling out evil spirits in the front yard, it will look like as if I am doing mime. Therefore, to prevent misunderstanding, I restrained myself when people were present and removed the evil spirits when I was alone. But sometimes I was caught by people passing by, and they looked at me strangely.

Tickling

The small and weak evil spirits attached to the outside of the body usually stay still, but they can tickle even with a little energy, and a little stronger spirits can cause pain. In general, few people feel the forces inside them. However, if saints become spiritually clean through thorough repentance, they can feel and be aware of the existence of even small spirits. People often get their hands on the spots where there is an evil spirit because they feel itchy. Those who do not feel the evil forces entering and leaving the body are because they already have too many evil spirits. Sometimes, there are some who do not feel the evil spirits among clean people; this is due to their lack of the gift of discernment.

Sticky

In summer, evil spirits are sticky because the weather is hot. Evil spirits are also affected by the temperature of the material world. Because the head is one of the most sensitive parts of our bodies, it is very unpleasant if there are many evil spirits on the head; they feel like the melted bond flowing down. Even if I want to remove them by hands since they are way too sticky, it is hard to take them off. In addition, accumulated evil spirits that have entered the body a long time ago and evil spirits of those who lack repentance are also very sticky.

To escape from the evil spirits that took hold of me, I have divided sins written in the scripture into twenty categories and repented each sin for a month. For those who read this book, I would like to introduce how I repented for each sin.

1. Pride

Father God! You are the owner of all creations. The only God, the highest, who deserves all glory. Yet I was full of pride from childhood. I denied your existence, and I did not seek you. Later, even though I accepted Jesus Christ as my Lord, I lived as though I am still the Lord of my life. Instead of living a Christ-centered life, I lived a self-centered life. Even as I was doing your work, I did it with the attitude of self-righteousness. Instead of seeking your kingdom, I put my plans and goals first. Rather than following your guidance, I did everything according to my plans and wants. Instead of depending on the Holy Spirit, I used secular and humanly methods; I relied on my own strengths and abilities.

Father God, I disobeyed you. I obeyed when the task given to me was favorable, and if the task was difficult, I avoided it and disobeyed you. You said partial obedience is the same as total disobedience. I developed a habit of making excuses and doing only the things that I want to do. I habitually disobeyed you, rebelled against you, and despised you. I did not die to myself before you and others; I have not put off the old self.

Father God! You said that pride goes before destruction, yet I have been prideful. King Saul of Israel was also a notable person but was abandoned for being prideful. Even while knowing this, I became prideful. What makes my sin greater is the fact that I was not aware of my pride. I sought to receive glory and honor together with you, and sometimes I robbed your credit and took it as my own. I often used you for my purpose, and when it did not turn out as my expectation, I blamed and slandered you.

Even when I was suffering the consequences of my sins, I did not repent but instead shifted the blames to others. I was boastful, showy, impudent, snobbish, rude, self-conceited, blowing my own horn, trusting my abilities, looks, experiences, and knowledge. I judged others with my standard; I despised, condemned, and controlled other people. I fell into spiritual superiority and became blind to the truth. I hated being instructed and criticized by others while I like to point out others' shortcomings and teach them. I criticized other communities and churches' problems while thinking I do not have the same issues. Father God, help me to be a humble and obedient servant who trusts you completely. Please, forgive me for all my pride.

My head ached when I repented for being arrogant; I felt a pain like a needle coming through my head. The spirits of arrogance descended from the head to the back of the neck and were connected to the shoulders. Countless small spirits kept coming out when I repented of my pride according to the timeline. Since I have been arrogant thousands and tens of thousands of times throughout my life, I had to repent as much as I have sinned.

2. Lust

Father God! I am lustful and have fallen short of your glory. I became entangled by the spirit of lust and worldly filth. I enjoyed obscene talks and adulterous shows. I used the media to inflame carnal desires. I intently looked at the scandals and intimate life stories. I liked to search for news that dealt with sexual issues. I was carelessly ensnared by my curiosity in the opposite sex. I tried to attract the opposite sex with flattery and appearance. I did not treat everyone equally but showed favoritism to the opposite sex, treating them nicer and showing them interest. I judged people according to their looks and dwelt on lustful thoughts.

I became addicted to physical pleasures and substance use. I enjoyed the pornographic materials. I entertained sexual perversions such as homosexuality, bestiality, rape, incest, extramarital affair, prostitution, voyeurism, other sexual perversions, concubinage, and premarital relationship, compulsive masturbation, pornographic videos, pictures, novels, and magazines.

As a child of God, I should have loved and revered the Lord more than anything. Yet I loved materials, spouse, children, friends, dates, celebrities, reputation, fame, popularity, authority, power, titles, influence, knowledge, skills, hobbies, and pleasure more than you. My mind and body, which belong to the Lord, were given in to the love of the world: to TV shows, dramas, movies, animations, games, sports, recreations, leisures, smart-phones, and computers. I was lustful since childhood. I am more adulterous than Gomer. Forgive me of all these sins.

When I repented for such lewdness, I felt a prick in my chest, and a thin evil spirits left me. Also, I felt itchy in the lower abdomen as if earthworms were wriggling. When my body reacted strangely, I was nervous at first, but I soon realized that these were the symptoms of evil spirits leaving my body. Every time I lust for something, I felt a thin spirit crawling into my lower abdomen.

3. Falsehood

Father God! The devil is the father of lies, yet, as though I was a child of the devil, I lied and acted deceitfully. God, I am double-faced and double-minded. I do not know you or your word very well, yet I acted as though I do and taught things that I do not understand very well. I am a false prophet in practice and a swindler. I decorated myself with falsehood, and I am full of false identities.

I falsely swore before you and other people; I added and subtracted your words; I defiled my mouth and tongue with flattery and lies; I used your name to propagate specific deceptive ideas; I harmed the neighbors through false accusations. I failed to acknowledge the truths. I falsely slandered others; I created rumors; I flattered and showed favoritism to my advantage; I requested others to lie; I changed my words and made others fall into a snare; I distorted the truth and mixed it with falsity. The authority of my lips was reduced as a result of my deceitfulness.

I falsely complimented those around me to win their favor. I made excuses saying to survive in this world, lying and exaggerations are inevitable. Lying became a natural tendency. When my lie was discovered, I did not confess the truth and apologize but instead made excuses to hide my faults and added further lies to escape the pinch. I fell into the deception of evolution and all kinds of other heretical teachings. I paid attention to misleading theologies and theories. I listened to the deceiving and condemning voices of the devil. I lacked the knowledge of God. Please, forgive me for all these sins.

As I repented all sorts of falsehood, many small forces came out from my gum, tongue, and lips. I had a stiff neck before, but now it feels soft and light.

4. Depression

Father God! Even though I claim to be your child, I lived powerlessly in depression and dissatisfaction. I lost interest in all things. I felt as though all things are meaningless. I lived in guilt, lethargy, and passivity, barely getting any things done. I was anxious and worried; I was tired of life; I fell into nihilism. I lost self-esteem, falling into inferiority complex and social anxiety. Sometimes I could not adapt to the world but rather feared it. I fell into a negative perception of self, a sense of emptiness, hopelessness, grief, loneliness, and self-criticism. I became exhausted, and I overslept. I became stressed with needless worries and over-thinking, so I suffered headaches, indigestion, and insomnia.

God, I was easily frustrated and irritated. I experienced a reduction in appetite, memory, concentration, thought process speed, passion, vitality, work efficiency, and performance. I neglected my duties, and I did it begrudgingly out of obligation. I could not adapt flexibly to the situation changes and deal successfully with exams, interviews, new jobs, loss of employment, retirement, marriage, end of relationships, and bereavement. I became disappointed, depressed, unhappy, and bitter. This was due to my distrust and self-reliance. Also, it is the result of my spiritual adultery and my ancestors. Now I believe that You, Lord, is my only solution. Please, forgive me for all these sins.

I felt a pain in my chest as I repented for depression. So I pressed or tapped my chest with my hands. When I repented my depression, many evil spirits came out of my lungs. The man of God must always rejoice in him.

5. Envy, Jealousy

Father God! Even though envy and jealousy are great sins that harm our body and hinder God's glory, I have committed the sin of envy and jealousy. I was displeased with the promotions of others. When I saw others passionately serving, offering, and receiving recognition, I became envious. Even though I know that God always sees everything about me, I became oblivious of God and became conscious of others. Sometimes I became envious and jealous without knowing why. Having an inferiority complex, I considered the coworkers of the kingdom as rivals and enemies. Greed, pride, and self-love filled my heart. I did not know my place, and I criticized and slandered the coworkers. When things did not go well for them, I secretly rejoiced. I did the work of God with flesh and fleshly desires.

I enjoyed being esteemed by people, and I was relieved when others complimented my deeds or performances. I tried to assume every position that would receive recognition of people. Envy and jealousy are forms of self-abuse, but I could not control it. Because of envy and jealousy, I became narrow-minded, and I could not easily accept and understand others. I judged your servants. I rejected, obstructed, opposed, criticized, and slandered them all out of envy, self-righteousness, and jealousy. A child of God should rejoice when the coworkers bear much fruit and do great exploits for the Lord's Kingdom. But I was unable to congratulate them and rejoice with them wholeheartedly. Please, forgive me for all these sins.

When I repented for my envy and jealousy, I felt pain in my lower abdomen because many evil spirits moved simultaneously. There is an old Korean proverb: "When a cousin purchase land, my stomach aches." I found it totally right spiritually.

6. Anger, Rage

Father God! I was full of rage and have fallen short of your glory. I was angry whenever things did not match my standards. I complained against you, blamed, opposed, and disobeyed You. Even though rage hinders grace, I grew impatient and angry and became an obstacle to the fulfillment of your righteousness. Sometimes

GO THROUGH REPENTANCE AGAIN

my blood rushed in rage. I was full of bitterness, frustration, and ill-temper. I was shouting and fuming with my face hot and red. The surge of rage that I suppressed would explode in time. I attempted to control it without success, becoming even bitter. When I held the anger in, I thought the anger would go away, but it was only accumulating inside of me. I confess that I did not die to myself before you and others. I could not lay myself down and be refined by your words. I could not let go of the grudges and hatred toward those that I considered as my enemies. I felt hurt and unfairly treated. If it did not match my standards, I argued and nitpicked. I stubbornly unyielded, continually complaining and troubling others.

I was smiling outside while hiding a venomous knife inside; I fretted, frowned, and shouted about insignificant things; I became vicious, cold-blooded, and intimidating to others. At times, I threw or broke objects, and I even hit others. I got agitated easily. I attacked others first, and I retaliated. I hurt my family and others around me with my blood rage. I cursed others and wished their downfall, even death. Sometimes, I was angry at myself, despising, and punishing myself. I looked at the world negatively and uttered a death wish. I became hateful and critical of myself, others, and the world. Please, forgive me for all these sins.

I was startled when I repented rage—a fist-sized evil spirit around the stomach area came up through my throat. Also, my back neck hurt so much. I felt a lot of strain in my shoulders. I had a stiff neck because I was very hot-tempered. Every time I got angry, these related evil spirits attacked me. People who often go into a rage and anger like me must repent for a very long time before they can be released.

7. Worry, Anxiety

Father God! I call myself a child of God. Yet I doubted your power and help, so I looked at the circumstances and worried. I could not let go of the heavy burdens to you, Lord, and I tried to carry it all by myself. I could not trust in your love and your promises that you will take all our burdens. Even though I am powerless without you, I am a fool who tries to live by my strengths and wisdom. I depended on other people.

I worried about what to eat and wear. Even though worrying is a great sin that harms my body and bones, I needlessly worried in anticipation and became anxious. I needlessly increased my sufferings and burdens by worrying. I fell into needless worries as a result of laziness. I felt like I should be doing something all the time, making myself always busy, restless, and tired. My mind became dull because of life's worries, fears, and anxiety, and the word of God could not bear much fruit in me as a result. I should be doing your work wholeheartedly with joy, But instead, I have made it an obligation and a burden. Even though I cannot gain anything by worrying, even while I knew this, I worried. Please, forgive me for all these sins.

I felt my heart refreshed when I repented for worrying and concerning. I sometimes tapped my chest with my hands because I felt like my heart was swelling, and it made me anxious. It turned out later that this phenomenon appeared because a lot of evil spirits came out of my heart at the same time.

8. Complaint, Ungratefulness

Father God! I am your child, yet I have not been godly with my words. I have complained and murmured many times. I could not recognize your absolute sovereignty in all things, and whenever the situations differed from my plans or expectations, I complained and made excuses not to get involved. I misunderstood and misjudged your words, so I rejected them, saying it is not what I want. I complained against you and blamed you for everything. I was not satisfied with my circumstances, so I resented you, and I resented the world. When things worked out well, I thanked you, but I complained when things did not go well.

I could not wait in patience, but I became anxious. Continual grumbling and complaining became a habit of mine. Even in my relationship with others, whenever I was let down, I complained and became bitter. I did not work with joy but with complaints and grumbling. I tormented others with my murmuring and grumbling. Even though you have given me so many things, I did not thank you for them, but instead, I looked at what I did not have and complained. Even though I am a person with many faults and weaknesses, I looked at others' faults and imperfections and complained about it. I could not accept and understand others with a wide heart. I was often sulky, murmuring whenever I opened my lips. Please, forgive me for all these sins.

The spirit of complaint and discontent were mainly in my throat and mouth, and when these spirits left, I felt fresh and cool.

9. Entertainment, Pleasure Seeking

Father God! Although I am living in this world, my purpose is to do God's work as a servant of God. But I sought after the pleasures of this world. I lived as though experiencing pleasure and being entertained is the goal of my life. I sought delicious foods, marvelous sights, leisure, and entertainment. I loved my hobby more than

God, spending much time on the internet, games, sports, traveling, SNS, cartoons, movies, television shows, dramas, music, and smartphone applications. I neglected my spiritual growth because of my addiction to media and entertainment. I failed my duties and purposes.

I became uninterested in society or other persons because I became absorbed in the entertainments and personal interests. I let my animal nature take control. I also enjoyed accumulating secular knowledge that has nothing to do with you, God. I did not desire eternity more than I desired the world. I did not know that true happiness comes from my relationship with you. You are my true joy and my all. Please, forgive me for all my sins.

I really struggled to live right before God, but I realized that I still have not neglected the world completely.

10. Alcohol

My ancestors became addicted to alcohol; they participated in drinking customs and competitions; they enjoyed the atmosphere. They used the effects of the drinks to be merry, to sing out loud, fight with others, and say things that they could not say without alcohol. They are alcohol addicts. They gave their family a hard time with the effects of alcohol. Please forgive them for all their sins.

Although I never had drunk alcohol, I heard that my maternal grandfather loved to drink. Since his blood flows in me, I repented his sin as my sin, and it worked.

11. Entertainment

Lord, I preferred to meet people, eat, and spend time outside when I had the opportunity, rather than doing your work faithfully. I liked to go out for air or travel around. I was envious of people going abroad, and I was excited when I had a chance to go out. Although I was departing for the ministry, I had a desire for amusement in the innermost recesses of the heart. Please forgive me.

I reproached people indulged in worldly entertainment, but sometimes I liked how free-spirited they were. I also enjoyed eating and playing. Israel and Rome fell because of pleasure-seeking, entertainment, and adultery; but I also partly participated in them. I wished to live holy and exemplary before you, but my life did not measure up to your standard. Have mercy on me and forgive me for all my sins.

12. Laziness

Father God! I should have served you with passion and diligence, yet I became lazy and unfaithful. I hindered your glory because of my laziness. Even though You wanted to use me for your work, I delayed and even spoiled it because I did not respond immediately. Bible study, sermon preparation, prayer, looking after the congregation, seeking God, and growing spiritually... I became lazy and lost fervor in all these things. I could not help others diligently. I expected good fortune without putting in any effort. I wasted the precious time you gave me, being a conformist who settles down for the present situations, merry-making, oversleeping, creating extra works for others, procrastinating, and making excuses. Also, avoiding jobs that I do not want to do or doing it reluctantly and without care. Even though I have many things to pray about, I did not ask, seek, and knock because of laziness. Although I did not spare my time and efforts with fun and worldly activities, I was lazy with my relationship with you and your works. I did not faithfully fulfill my promises to you and others. I led a life unworthy of your grace. My lazy acts and attitudes brought loss to my community, and I failed to receive God's approval and others. I did not participate and serve in the community out of my laziness, and I became isolated as a result. My laziness caused a vicious cycle of crumbling economic status. Please forgive me for all these sins.

13. Doubt

Father God! I hindered the glory of God through my doubt and unbelief. Even though I believe in a creator God, I did not believe in a sustaining and intervening God. I could not believe the love of God as well as the judgment and the wrath of God. I thought myself to be a child of God, but I could not believe that I have the authority as your child. I could not rely on the blessings and provisions of God. Even though living according to your words leads to great blessings, I could not live according to it.

When I was desperate, I sought after you, but I forgot about you when I was abundant. Even though I believe in you, the almighty God, I have a shallow faith that worries continuously. I have a weak faith that does not testify to God with boldness. I have a dead faith that believes with words but not with acts.

I lacked assurance in your love and promises. I did not listen to and respect the teachings and the advice that I received through your servants. Even though God's power and authority manifest in the present day and many people testify about your living presence, miracles, and wonders, I could not experience them in my life due to lack of faith. When I faithfully obey and follow your path, you promised to repay me in a hundred-fold in this life and the next life, but I often lost my faith on the way. Please, forgive me for all these sins.

14. Stinginess

Father God! I hindered your glory through my stinginess. I was generous to myself but stingy to you and others. I ignored the weak and needy. I gave reluctantly, sparingly, and I expected and demanded credit for what I have done. I carefully calculated to maximize the credit I would receive. I gave reluctantly, but I received joyfully. Because of my stinginess, I have not given much to you who has given everything to me. Because of my lack of giving to you and my neighbors, I could not receive your financial blessing but rather became ensnared by the spirit of poverty.

Even though everything in this world is yours, I considered my properties as my own. Although tithing is a proclamation that everything I have is yours, I skipped giving it. I gave it without joy and thanksgiving. I gave it reluctantly, out of custom and obligation. Not only in financial matters but also in giving compliments, thanksgiving, and doing good works, I was stingy. I am ungenerous and selfish. I was rich and generous in giving criticisms and condemnations. As a result, I am poor and destitute physically and spiritually. Now I decide to be generous to you and my neighbors. Please, give me the grace to make this change in my life. Help me walk the path that You walked, the path of generosity even to sacrificial giving of self and unconditional love. Forgive me of all my sins.

15. Fear

Father God! You love and protect me, but I could not fully embrace peace and freedom by faith. I could not entrust my life and properties to you, and I hindered God's glory by fearing the people and the world. I doubted the promises of God. By committing sins, I permitted the fear to come into my mind. I forgot about

God because of my fear of people and the circumstances. I feared your call, so I could not move forward. I could not boldly proclaim the truth and preach the gospel because of my fear of people and public speaking. You told us to be bold, but I became passive and small-minded.

I could not follow you faithfully because of my fear of death and suffering, fear of people's opinions and judgments, fear of instability. I could not freely walk according to my uncompromised faith. I became conscious of how people look at me. Because of the fear of failure, I could not step forward boldly. When I met someone with greater stature, strength, knowledge, degree, title, fame, and wealth, I was intimidated. I was also intimidated by the number of people.

We would experience God's love as we draw near you, but I considered you a fearful God, and I considered it a fearful thing to approach you because of my shortcomings. The truth is that the more my weaknesses, the more I should draw near to you, and the more abundant is your grace that covers me and transforms me. The enemy of Israel was not only Canaanites but also the Israelites who feared the war and committed the sin of unbelief. In the same way, I committed the sin of unbelief and became full of fear. Please forgive me for all these sins.

16. Greed

Father God! I hindered your glory with my former ways of life, my old self, corrupt with deceitful desires of the world. I am full of greed, vanity, and carnal desires. Even though I say I do the work of God, I was doing it, subconsciously, for my personal gains. I used you, God, for my selfish desires. I envied those who have more than I do. I delighted in people's recognition and respect; I assumed positions beyond my place and brought misfortune upon myself; I suffered great losses, spiritually and physically, as a result.

With competition and rivalry, I harmed the relationships with my brothers and sisters in Christ, whom I was supposed to love and accept. I possessed too much, and I spent extravagantly. I always tried to do things excessively, show myself off, do many things, and receive much recognition, sometimes beyond my physical limitations. But even with all that, I felt empty and dissatisfied, as if something is missing. Instead of handing it to others and building them up, I grasped it for myself. I snatched it from their hands. The grass looked greener on the other side. I envied what others have and not be content with the sufficient grace I already received.

I was not considerate of others but only selfish and self-serving. If I see something that I like, I had to make it mine to be satisfied. I accumulated and possessed more than what is necessary. I was obsessed with having more than others and possessing expensive brand items to show off. I became delighted and satisfied with worldly possessions, fame, and success. Lord, I will seek and desire the things above and put my joy and hope in heaven. Please forgive me for all these sins.

17. Impatience

Father God! I have become impatient and hasty and hindered the glory of God. I went ahead of your Spirit and your will, not being able to wait patiently for your work and promises to be fulfilled in its time. When my plans did not go as I willed or delayed, I blamed you and complained against you. I did not wait for your confirmation or blessings, but I made my plans and acted according to my own flesh and desires, and I became all anxious when the goals were not achieved or delayed. I acted out of my place and lacked self-control.

Even though God sovereignly decides everything and makes everything beautiful in its time, I distrusted you, and I put myself in your position by hastily judging. I prayed shallowly out of habit, and I demanded quick answers. I was swayed by people's opinions and fell into pit-falls. I could not discern God's perfect will. I entangled myself by making empty promises and big-talks. I acted hastily and spoiled many things. Even though I lacked understanding, I misrepresented others before they spoke for themselves. I could not let go of all things to you.

I tried to sow my seeds and create my own fruits. I did not plant the seeds because I hated waiting for the fruits. I harvested the fruits prematurely out of impatience. I tried to achieve everything quickly by human methods; I could not wait for your time and receive the full blessing; I could not patiently wait for the unrepentant brothers and family members. I got angry at my offenders before they had a chance to repent and apologize. I quickly judged others without fully understanding their problems and their situations. Please, forgive me for all these sins.

18. Disclosure

Father God! You called me to be a counselor and a consultant who must have heavy lips guarding others' secrets and must not be quick to judge or belittle others. Yet I have let out some secrets and failed to protect them. When my relationship with them did not go well, I subtlely let out their faults and sins to others. I often enjoyed fault-finding in others. I boasted about having found others' secrets, and I told my friends: "this is a secret, but…" I was not faithful and wise. I mentioned others' faults to hide my flaws. I justified myself, defended myself, excused myself while defaming others in the process.

I could not stand not telling someone about a secret I learned. Letting out a secret came back to me like a boomerang. Sometimes I intentionally let known a good work that I have done in secret to boast about myself and receive recognitions. Sometimes, things went out of hand due to the words that I let out, and I panicked and regretted over the spilled milk is my duty to cover the sins and the faults of others, yet I have done the opposite. I gossiped and harmed the community. Then I defended and justified myself, saying it was an act of justice. Sometimes I used others' secrets to my advantage.

Lord, I will only talk about good things about others. I will only spread the gospel and boast about you and your works. Please forgive me for all these sins.

19. Chatter

Father God! I have committed too many sins with my mouth. I slandered others, cursed, shouted, let out secrets and personal information, and started rumors, and I needlessly chattered. I wasted precious time you gave me with needless chatters. Whenever I had time, I gathered with people, whispered with them, and made idle talks and gossip. I scolded others, grumbled, told tales, hurt others' reputations, and harmed relationships by whispering, accusations, rumors, and slandering. I defamed others behind their backs. I provided unnecessary and malicious information. I tempted and misled others, talking them into taking sides.

I exaggerated. I flattered, enticed, and disguised to be loyal. My lips are unclean. It is filthy, and both the sweet and the bitter water come out of it. I judged, criticized, condemned, slandered, and found faults. I made sarcastic jokes that bear thorns of criticism. I loved to talk more than to listen. I talked out of my turn - intruding and taking control of the conversations. I continually boasted so to receive recognition of others. I could not control my lips and continuously uttered unnecessary things.

Sometimes I said things that I should not have said and caused troubles for myself and others. You said to not associate with anyone whose mouth is always open and whose lips are hasty. You said without gossip, a quarrel dies down. I am the chatter and the gossip who has caused many unnecessary disputes. I let many words out of my mouth, but I am ashamed about what kinds of fruits and the number of fruits my words have borne.

Now I decide only to encourage and build others, speak the truth that saves souls, give life, and express love. Let my lips be the fountain of life by your grace. Please forgive me for all my sins.

20. Nicotine

Lord, I hardly smoked, but I thought those who smoke very cool when I was young. The smell of cigarettes was unpleasant, but the smell felt good occasionally. I used to hang out with smokers. Although I did not smoke, I entered the smoking areas and received nicotine into my body. Our ancestors smoked, and nicotine could be in my body a little bit. Lord, please keep me clean and forgive me.

I prayed with the list of these twenty sins and checked how many percent of each sin remained in my body. There is not only one big evil spirit in the human body; there are thousands or tens of thousands of evil spirits, ranging in size from very small to quite large.

There is not much difference in the number of sins people commit, except for those who have great evil spirits in particular.

GO THROUGH REPENTANCE AGAIN

To assume that the forces in the unrepented people's body are set at 100%, after repenting and receiving deliverance ministry from a competent minister for a month, one can generally remove about 50% of the evil spirits in the body. Yet it varies depending on the sincerity of repentance and the number of evil spirits one had before.

If the saints sincerely repent the sins that have the most significant impact on their lives one more time, an additional 10 to 15% of the evil spirits leave on average. At this rate, a few large forces remain in the body; to be more accurate, only evil spirits less than 2 centimeters in diameter remain.

When the evil spirits that remain in the body of the saints fall below 30%, Satan and his followers have difficulty in overturning them. Evil spirits depart only when saints exactly repent and sincerely turn back from their sins. Therefore, it is most effective to repent while seeing the past sins through the visions or the gift of the word of wisdom. If saints continue to repent for a year or so in this way, evil spirits in the body will fall below 10 to 20%. In my experience, those who have less than 20% of evil spirits in their bodies can be truly called "saints." Anyone who wants to fall below 10% needs to pray for another six months or a year. Those who have reached this level are a minority; only those who strive for holiness, intimate relationship with the Lord, and self-denial can push themselves hard up to here.

To make evil spirits in the body less than 5%, saints must stop everything for about two years and concentrate only on repentance. But no matter how hard they pray, humans can not become utterly clean. I tried to clear out all the sins for a long time, yet arrogance and lust never fell below 1 to 2%. I asked the Lord why and he replied, "No matter how thoroughly you repent and how holy you become, as long as you are in the flesh, you will always have these two issues." When I heard him, I realized once again that every one of us is a "sinner."

We should avoid criticizing each other for this reason. Repentance makes me feel like I am the worst sinner. Remember that Paul also confessed that he was the greatest sinner of all (Tim. 1:15).

Repentance draws people away from their interest in gossiping with others. Since the Holy Spirit allowed me a broken and contrite heart, I cried every night for five years and confessed, "Lord, here's the sinner." The thought of standing before the Lord, in the end, brought tears to my eyes.

I got off work at 11 p.m. on average for five to six years. I only stayed in the church every day, so I did not even notice the seasons changing. Although I lived in a big city, Seoul, I lived like a monk in the desert. I lived just praying like this at the age when I should bear the most fruit of my ministry, but I never thought it was a waste of time. I was grateful and satisfied just to be able to provide spiritual help to other saints.

For the great grace of God and the blessing he gave me, I thought I could obey even if God asked me to go into the mountains and live the rest of my life there, and I still have the same passion today.

PART 5

EXPANSION OF MINISTRY

CHAPTER 23

BEGIN TO EXPLORE SPIRITUAL SITES

I saw evil spirits in the body of man, and evil spirits in the house, in the church, and in the public facilities, but I was not satisfied. I decided to tour the three most famous village shrines in Seoul, referring to the book *Korean Exorcism and Shamans,* written by Ru-Si Hwang. I could not bear to wonder how full the place would be of evil spirits. I was very busy with the healing ministry, but I visited the shrine sites several times with a few disciples whose spiritual eyes are opened.

First, I visited the village shrine in Naksan, Jongno-gu. This place has been reorganized as a park, so there was no trace of a shrine. Yet we selected a few high places with big trees as candidates. As we spiritually diagnosed each spot, we finally found a place with great evil spirits. My disciples and I drew the evil spirits respectively and shared with each other afterward. This tour became the very first step of studying the territorial or regional spirits of Korea.

When it comes to making spiritual maps, people usually think of it as locating and organizing sacred places. However, we made a spiritual map by revealing the evil spirits that are invisible to ordinary people.

The second village shrine we toured was in Ssamji Park, Dapsimni. As soon as we entered the park, young students in the group were overwhelmed by the giant spirits and were afraid to go in further because they immediately had a headache. The energy of evil spirits in this place was much stronger than Naksan because of the great number of huge evil spirits. As far as I know, the residents of this area held a shaman ritual every year.

As I mentioned earlier, I spent my childhood in this town. I lived next door to the shrine when I was in elementary school. Even after moving a little away from here, I still came back to play in the trees. Sometimes, I broke branches and ran away. I had no idea that this place would have so many evil spirits as one of Seoul's three great shrines. It turned out that I played with friends among these strong forces.

Lastly, my disciples and I went to Sangbong-dong, which is close to Tae-neung, a tomb area of a queen from the Josun Dynasty. The site was famous for shaman rituals; many received evil spirits here. Consequently, there were many spirits as we expected, but it was different from the other two places in that evil forces were stretched up to the sky, and there was another great spirit moving on top of them. Knowing this spiritual reality will help everyone to stay alert and realize how formidable spiritual war is.

At another time, we toured the places where famous shamans perform exorcisms. Professional shamans have great skills because they serve strong evil spirits as their masters. We have accumulated a lot of spiritual information by touring around many places.

I had a desire to make research on the Korean church spiritually. The Lord also visited the seven churches in the Book of Revelation and examined each church. Some of them were praised, some were condemned, and some were praised and condemned at the same time.

My disciples and I analyzed various churches in dozens of ways. Some churches were as good as we expected, but some were short of our expectations. Honestly, I was disappointed with many of the leading churches in Korea. Since we were accord in our spiritual diagnosis, my disciples and I could have confidence in our spiritual mapping.

While studying Korean churches, I thought that the Lord would also evaluate us from various angles. We live in the end time where Satan and his followers possess great power, therefore, the church must pray instead of promoting fellowship by going picnic. I wish many churches would pull themselves together and turn into battle formation.

I got very excited every time I added a new place to spiritual mapping. It is essential to study the distribution of evil spirits in order to gain the upper hand in the fight. Also, I wanted to know the spiritual environment of Korea precisely. With dozens of people, I searched for places where evil spirits might work powerfully and tried to take over the place spiritually to bring it under God's reign again. We made a visit to various locations in Korea for about three to four times a year, which cost quite a lot of money. Yet, I invested a lot of money for this task regardless of the cost.

In the beginning, I went around with young disciples whose spiritual eyes are wide opened, but afterward, I went to the famous mountains of Korea with many capable pastors. In particular, we visited Taebaek Mountain, Mani Mountain, Jiri Mountain, and Gyeryong Mountain, which were considered as "spiritual mountains" from ancient times. We also visited temples that are thousands of years old at home and abroad to study the overall spiritual condition. I believe there will be an opportunity to share the details in the future.

CHAPTER 24

START A LIVE BIBLE STUDY

Many changes have occurred to me as I began to see the spiritual world. Among them, the most significant change was my perspective of reading the Bible. I entered the seminary at 20 years old and read the Bible countless times. I also read many commentaries, preached, and taught many people for 30 years. Pastors who have been pastoring for more than 20 years would be proud to know a certain degree of the Bible.

Since I loved the word of God and kept myself close to the word, I, like other pastors, believed that I was at least a half expert. But when I opened my spiritual eyes and read the Bible in the Holy Spirit, I realized spiritual things that I had not known before. Despite my broad background knowledge of the Bible, things that were never heard of or seen elsewhere have popped out of the Bible. For the past few years, every time I read the Bible, I experienced the same experience, which made me thrilled to open the word of the Lord.

Whenever I realized the word anew, I was grateful, but on the one hand, I was embarrassed. I tried to study the Bible in the original language to understand better, however, since I was not used to the language, it took me a lot of time. Reading the Bible from the whole another level now, I realized that despite my utmost attempt to digest the word, the knowledge I had previously acquired was quite insufficient. There were also quite a few parts that were preached superficially, barely revealing the meaning of the biblical text.

I was ashamed before the Lord, and I felt sorry for the countless saints who had listened to my sermons and teachings. This scruple of conscience had grown so great that I could not look into the eyes of my former saints who came to see me, and it is still hard for me to face them.

The Bible was written by the anointed prophets and disciples of Jesus with the inspiration of the Holy Spirit. Therefore, the key to properly comprehend the Bible is to be filled with the Holy Spirit. Of course, background knowledge such as language, history, culture, and author's life are also essential factors in the interpretation of the Bible. Yet no one will deny that the enlightening of the Holy Spirit is the most critical one. Bible researchers and pastors cannot be unaware of this fact. However, since "filled with the Holy Spirit" means different to each people and it is difficult to measure the fullness of the Holy Spirit, only a few people will continuously strive to reach a deeper level.

For I had theological education from great teachers, and my library was full of commentaries and studies, I was confident in the interpretation of the Bible. But this pride of mine was shattered in an instant. The walls of knowledge that I had previously accumulated fell apart as I walked with the Holy Spirit closely and understood the spiritual world. Yet it does now mean that I deny everything I have known before. I tried my best to draw the meaning out of the text, but it was too shallow, and some were even wrong.

The word of the Lord is perfect and flawless, but interpreters, oftentimes, distorted the Bible by having either an excessively rational and reasonable perspective or overly symbolic and spiritual perspective. Everybody faces some limitations when interpreting the Bible, so I carefully considered this issue and came up with three solutions for myself:

1. Get over my partial theological knowledge for the time being.
2. Consider my previous reading as a reference laying the groundwork.
3. Let the Bible speak and listen to it humbly.

Instead of studying the Bible with various tools, I decided to listen carefully to what the word reveals to me, and I was impressed every time. Although I had read the Bible countless times, new spiritual aspects were highlighted to my eyes as I listened to the Holy Spirit. Just by reading the word, I could feel the atmosphere at the time the Bible was recorded and realized why God had said so in what sense. It was a surprising and just amazing experience.

Facts or secrets that I came to know were things I had never discovered before. I did not enjoy this myself; I prepared sermons with new revelations and preached it on Sunday. The congregation and other pastors were touched by them. There may be few problems when evaluating my sermons from a preaching point of view, but everyone gladly accepted and acknowledged the word of God revealed through me. Since the meaning of the text was easily grasped, I needed less time to prepare sermons. No matter what text I choose to preach, God's word spoke to me through the Holy Spirit.

I began to read the Bible again from Genesis. I did an in-depth study of 200 characters in the Bible, and I re-studied and preached the Gospels again. Time flew so fast because it was exciting and pleasant to read God's word. I named my new way of studying the Bible "Live Bible Research" because the word came to me vividly as if it were alive. I held seminars and presented my research, and helped pastors who wanted to know the Bible deeper. I have held ten seminars so far.

I plan to continue to exposit the word of God. Many books already released in the market will serve as the foundation, but the Holy Spirit will add fresh and a more profound revelation on to it.

CHAPTER 25

DEVELOP VARIOUS SPIRITUAL DIAGNOSTIC TOOLS

The spiritual condition of each believer was very different, and the Lord taught me case by case. Various spiritual diagnostic tools have been developed naturally in this way to help numerous saints. I instructed those who came for training with what I learned from the Lord. I am delighted to see so many gifted people with spiritual abilities at this age. I would like to introduce some pieces of training in this chapter.

1. Way to Heaven
This is a spiritual diagnosis to figure out whether a saint is making good progress toward heaven. I can see what blessings God gave to each person, and at the same time, what forces hinder the person from pushing forward. This ministry reminds me of John Bunyan's *Pilgrim's Progress*.

2. Marital relationship
This is a ministry to check how couples are doing now. I can see how much they love each other and how much they expect from

each other. In addition, I can analyze whether or not the relationship is well balanced overall.; if not, I can also analyze the cause.

3. How well am I doing?

Through this ministry, I can see how much God loves a saint and how much he or she loves God. I can also figure out how much one prays, how much material one gives, and whether the dedication of a saint measures up to God's expectation or not.

4. The Color of Spirituality

Heaven is full of beautiful colors. Likewise, the colors of the gift that the Holy Spirit gives to each person are also diverse. I see spirituality in blue, reverence in red, and power in yellow. This ministry enables a saint to understand what kind of gifts he or she has, and their characteristics in colors. If an individual's spiritual gifts appear in rainbow colors, it signifies an abundance of gifts, in other words, one has almost all the gifts in perfect balance.

5. Place in the Church

Each believer is a church and, at the same time, a member of the church. Therefore, every single saint is precious. Through this ministry, I can identify which part a believer belongs to and what kind of service or ministry that one is loyal to in the church.

6. Homes in Heaven

People who have experienced near-death or those whose spirits came out of the body sometimes go to heaven and see houses in heaven. However, if one's spiritual eyes are deeply open, one can see the homes in heaven without tasting death. I can see whether a house is prepared or not, the size of the house, and how much the house has been built. Although saints are saved and go to heaven, they are all rewarded differently because the Lord rewards each of them according to how they lived on the earth.

7. Calling

All of us are born with a mission or vocation. And knowingly or not, we live accordingly. Yet, some individuals are not confident about the given tasks. Through this ministry, people can verify their callings from the Lord.

8. Living Water

The Holy Spirit gives grace to all who are born again. The living water mostly comes in through the upper part of the head and through the lower abdomen. In particular, the Bible says that streams of living water flow from the innermost being or belly; only when the living water overflows, the soul can be in a good state with full of energy. Through this ministry, I can see whether the living water is smoothly supplied or if there is any blockage preventing the water from entering.

9. Spiritual Level

Believers must push themselves toward the throne of God. I can see what level the saints are at and what condition they are in. When setting the highest level of spirituality at ten, most people remain in the middle. Famous saints who earnestly seek the Lord in Korea seem to be in the 7th to 8th stages. Even among people in the same stage, their conditions vary: some are striving to go further; some are taking rest fully satisfied, and some are enjoying their current state.

10. What is the Cross?

All people, whether they want it or not, have at least a cross to carry, and the cross represents many things in this ministry: it can be parents, children, mission, finance, health, friends, etc. The size, shape, material, weight, and location of the cross all look different depending on the individual. As disciples of Jesus Christ, every believer should bear the cross and follow him.

As I became to see the spiritual world, I not only expelled evil spirits but also helped saints to walk in Christ. The Lord has taught me more than 150 tools to verify people's spiritual conditions. The Holy Spirit knows every aspect of each of us.

CHAPTER 26

FELLOWSHIP WITH SPIRITUAL PEOPLE

Through various channels, I knew that there are many people in Korea who are very close to God, including Pastor Doo-Sup Um, who founded Eunseong Abbey in Korea and wrote many spiritual books, Pastor In of Gapyeong, and Pastor Yun-Ho Lee, a disciple of Charles Kraft. I personally met some of them. Also, I took the time to attend spiritual meetings, and sometimes, I called people whom I wanted to get to know and had conversations over the phone.

I always longed to learn more because I had a flaming desire to know everything about the spiritual world. I studied great teachers at home and abroad and their influenced disciples. Influential figures always have at least one teacher who influenced their lives. Since the world is small, if you are willing, it is possible to reach or get reliable sources about people you are interested in.

I visited people I wanted to meet, and I also invited those whom I respected to my church to hold revival meetings.

Through Dr. Ho-Sik Kim, I learned the theory of angels and evil spirits. Through Reverend Sang-Tae Park, the publisher of the *Gospel of Christ,* I learned about a godly life. When I invited Dr.

Ronald Sawka, I gained knowledge of the prophetic ministry and how it can be utilized in the ministry.

Many men and women of God helped me to seek God and guided me to experience the spiritual world. Without them, I would not have grown to be the person I am now. I was not intensively influenced by a certain figure because I tried to learn and absorb everyone's strengths.

There is nothing that hinders growth more than building our own castle and settling in it, thinking that we have reached a certain level. I will not stop expecting to meet great ministers and have fellowship with them until the day the Lord comes back.

CHAPTER 27

BEGIN TO WRITE BOOKS

Trainee Writes a Book

Missionary Dong-Wook Kim came to my healing center and repented for a few weeks because the Holy Spirit led him to deep repentance. He cried every day in front of the church platform for three weeks. And based on that, he wrote a book called *The Prayer of Heaven*. This book is gaining popularity with many who desire to repent thoroughly. It is an honor for me to write a recommendation letter for this book.

Pastor Kwang-Wook Kim also wrote and distributed a book, *True Repentance Prayer* to help people repent of their idolatry and personal sins. Many people use this book because of its portability.

Start Writing Books
1. Heal My Lambs

It was heartbreaking to watch thousands of saints suffer under the evil spirits. As a result of the church's failure to teach the saints that evil spirits can build houses and settle in their bodies, they became ignorant of the tragic reality. These evil spirits residing in the bodies caused many problems afflicting people, yet most of the saints simply passed on as a test or platform that God had allowed. This book introduces 37 cases of selected people among those I ministered. I recorded various phenomena that appeared during the deliverance ministry and explained the main cause behind the scene.

I could have published this book a little earlier, but I waited and did not hurry until I was convinced of everything in this book. I also took the time to think about how to deal with the backlash and criticism of those who do not believe in the spiritual phenomena. However, I decided not to hold it any longer and introduce this book to the world since it has been seven years that I first opened my spiritual eyes and started spiritual ministry.

2. Jesus Christ and His Ministries

All pastors and saints will have desires to learn the word of God more profoundly. I published this book with the aim of helping the saints understand and grasp the Lord's ministry on another level. The book takes a deep look at the text related to the Lord in the gospel and deals with the study of the spiritual background and meaning of the ministry of Jesus Christ. In an attempt to redress the balance, I added vivid spiritual implication to the text because many existing books on biblical interpretations put more weight on the textual, historical, and cultural aspects of the text. I wrote this book on 52 subjects so that pastors can use it as a resource for Sunday sermons.

3. Biblical Spirituality

"What is spirituality?" This question is frequently asked by countless people of God, especially spiritual ones. This book covers the calling of each saint who is sent with a mission from heaven. It also deals with genuine repentance and the list of various sins.

Part 3, "The Bestowment of Power" describes the diverse gifts of the Holy Spirit that were manifested through the people of God from the Old Testament to the New Testament and from the Church Age to today. In particular, the gifts related to fighting Satan are very important. Saints whose spiritual eyes are opened can see the true nature of Satan. Quite a few pages are spent to explain the key to win the spiritual battle. The last part of the book covers walking with the Lord unto heaven, receiving praise from the Lord, and living a new life in heaven.

I wrote this book, hoping that it would become a textbook for "spirituality." Much of the content recorded in this book may not be easily found in other books. Although there is nothing new under the sun, there are things that the Lord reveals only in this era, and there are parts that people did not record on purpose.

4. Books to Write

I am preparing for my fifth book now, which will deal with how believers are suffering from Satan after losing their shepherd in the world. I am also planning to write a sequel to *Heal My Lambs* to introduce specific ministry details that unfold during the healing ministry.

As a sixth book, I would like to organize 150 spiritual state diagnostic tools mentioned earlier and publish them as a textbook for training spiritual gifts. I looked for books on how to train and develop spiritual gifts, yet I have not found any book on the market, so I am planning to write one for myself.

I also have a desire to publish an illustrated book depicting the distribution of evil spirits that lie in the human body. If this book comes out to the world, the identity of the evil spirits in us will be uncovered, and it will shock many people.

Lastly, I want to publish my research works from the Live Bible Study. This book will include a study of 200 biblical figures, and once people read it, they will see the Bible from a whole new perspective.

CHAPTER 28

ESTABLISH THE SILOAM HOUSE

Disciple Training in Small Size

Most people who repented and opened spiritual eyes through the Siloam Healing Center were pastors. They brought their children to the center to repent together, and they naturally recovered spiritual senses. Pastor's children have many advantages over their parents.

First, they already have a path of repentance, which their parents paved the way for them. Second, evil spirits passed down to the children easily lose their power when their parents repent. Third, since children are young, they have not sinned much yet, which means they have less evil spirits. For these reasons, evil spirits in the children leave relatively easily and quickly. Lastly, young children repent and receive spiritual training with an open heart because they have less bias toward spiritual experiences than their parents. As a consequence, they usually see the spiritual world well.

My wife and I decided to train the pastor's children for these reasons. They came to our center during the semester, but mostly, they were trained intensively during the vacation. Students living in rural areas came to Seoul and stayed with us for weeks. The young children trained in this way yielded good results.

Create a Two-Month Program of Training

To help those who repented and opened spiritual eyes to go deeper, a two-month intensive training program was created. Most of the trainees were pastors, and since they had their own church ministry, they could not thoroughly put a great amount of time only in spiritual training. They prayed for their sins for a month, and they were trained for another month.

I gave lectures, helped developing spiritual gifts, and trained people for deliverance ministry. It was impossible to learn everything in two months, but the program benefitted pastors in a way that they tasted the introductory level of spiritual ministry. Surprisingly, however, most pastors were satisfied at this stage and did not pursue further.

Siloam House

Fortunately, among the people who were trained at the center, the number of people who longed to learn more about the spiritual world gradually increased. I founded the Siloam House to meet the need of people and created an advanced training program. The Siloam House was established for the following purposes:

Currently, there are many aspects of Korean churches that deviate from the biblical church, and we feel that we are partly responsible for this.

1. In interpreting the Bible, the spiritual part has been overlooked or weakened, while the rational part has been overly emphasized. We will interpret the Bible correctly with the help of the Holy Spirit.

2. Korean churches often have more interest in expanding the power of the church rather than cherishing and saving souls. We will strive to love and build one soul.

3. When it is necessary to cultivate saints as holy as God, Korean churches have been producing saints who are barely going to heaven. We will help people to repent every day and become a pure bride of our Lord.

4. Although the kingdom of God is near, and it will be completed in heaven, the Korean church is building a castle on this earth. We aim to put our hearts only in heaven.

5. Korean churches are too insensitive to evil spirits when they are causing sickness and hindering saints from God's blessing. We will repent, fight sin, and do our utmost to win the spiritual battle.

Today is the age of spirituality, however, many churches remain complacent in the present and put their hopes on earthly things. In this reality, I hope that the Siloam House will serve as an institution that promotes the spiritual revival movement. It is my wish that this movement would go beyond the Keswick and L'Abri movement.

The Siloam House will give lectures on spiritual interpretation of the Old Testament and the New Testament, as well as systematic theology and church history.

We will continue to reveal the identity of evil spirits through spiritual mapping and fight spiritual battles against them. We will do our best to teach what true spirituality is by helping people explore the theory and practice of biblical spirituality.

The pastors delivering lectures at Siloam House are also

spirituals people who were trained here. They are very talented people with a bachelor's degree and a master's degree in theology. Also, they are well balanced between theories and practices because they have read numerous spiritual books.